The
5-Minute
BIBLE
STUDY
for
Teen Girls

ISBN 978-1-64352-435-1

Published by Barbour Books, an imprint of Barbour Publishing, Inc., 1810 Barbour Drive, Uhrichsville, Ohio 44683, www.barbourbooks.com

Our mission is to inspire the world with the life-changing message of the Bible.

Member of the
Evangelical Christian
Publishers Association

Printed in the United States of America.

The 5-Minute

BIBLE STUDY

for Teen Girls

Carey Scott

BARBOUR BOOKS
An Imprint of Barbour Publishing, Inc.

Introduction

Life is a full-time job, isn't it? Between school and sports, jobs and volunteering, family gatherings and friend time, it's hard to find the space to read the Bible. You may have every good intention, but life moves fast and before you know it, it's been days or weeks since you've spent time with God. This book makes it easy and quick to study His Word every day—even if you only have five minutes!

Minutes 1–2: **Read** the scripture passage for each day's Bible study.

Minute 3: **Understand.** Chew on a couple of thought-provoking statements that will challenge you and offer perspective in your own life.

Minute 4: *Apply.* Read a brief devotional that will help unpack the scripture passage and how it applies to your life today.

Minute 5: *Pray.* Use the sample prayer as-is or let it be a prompt as you talk to God. Don't forget to listen. He has things to say to you too.

The 5-Minute Bible Study for Teen Girls is the perfect way to dig into the Bible. His Word is alive and active, and relevant to your life right now. And even though you're a busy teen, finding five minutes of guided God time is doable! Even more, it will make a noticeable difference in your day and in your life.

Attention to Detail

Read Genesis 1:1–31

Key Verse:

Now the earth was formless and empty,
darkness was over the surface of the deep, and the
Spirit of God was hovering over the waters.
GENESIS 1:2 NIV

Understand:

- *Recognize the creative mind of God to*
  literally craft something from nothing.
  He took a formless and empty planet
  and brought it to life. Your creative God
  thought up a beautiful place for you.
  What part of the creation story intrigues
  you the most?
- *If God can think up and manage such*
  details, making something so spectacular
  from lifelessness, what keeps you from
  trusting Him to do the same in your life?

Apply:

Details matter to God. This first chapter in the
book of Genesis offers a glimpse into His thought
process. These thirty-one verses allow us a peek into
the mind of God, giving us the opportunity to see

His attention to detail.

He thought of everything. God lit up the darkness and populated the sky with stars, creating the moon and sun so seasons and days would exist. He broke up the water with land and created vegetation for beauty and as a food source. He designed birds to soar in the skies and fish to swim in the oceans. He created the regal lion and the animated monkey and every kind of animal in between. God thought of everything!

Maybe He included these details as an encouragement to you. Think about it. If God can manage every part of creation, maybe you can trust that He's able to manage every part of your life too.

Pray:

God, thank You for showing me how much You care about details. It helps me trust that if I will ask, You'll help manage every part of my life. Help me remember that You are willing to intervene, even in the messy moments. I need Your help to live my one and only life well. In Jesus' name I pray. Amen.

God Knows Your Needs

Read Genesis 2:1–25

Key Verse:

Thus the man chose names for domesticated animals, birds, and wild beasts. But none of these creatures was a right and proper partner for Adam.
GENESIS 2:20 VOICE

Understand:

- *Trust that God sees your needs. Even more, He cares about them. What are the top three things you desperately need in your life right now? Do you see God moving in those places yet?*
- *It was when Adam was sleeping that God took a rib and formed a woman. Adam wasn't responsible for meeting his own need. Instead, God let him rest as He created a solution. What would it look like for you to let God be God, and for you to trust Him to provide?*

Apply:

God breathed into the nostrils of Adam and it gave him life. He literally needed God's breath to come alive. God was the One who knew exactly what

Adam needed in that moment. And as time went on—maybe even before Adam was aware on his own—God recognized another need. Adam needed a partner.

God sees you. He knows exactly what your situations and circumstances require. He is fully aware of what troubles your heart and confuses your mind. God knows what you long for and what scares you. And in His sovereignty, God knows the exact moment you'll need His help.

Today, think about the places you need God's intervention. Tell Him what you're facing and where you are struggling. Let God know every part of your life that feels incomplete. It's not that He doesn't already know those places, but God loves when you share your heart with Him in prayer.

Pray:

God, what a relief to know You're already aware of every one of my needs. Sometimes I am too, but other times, I'm clueless. It's such a comfort that You see everything. Help me remember to share my heart with You. It's not always that I don't want to. So often, I just get busy and forget. But I believe You are for me always! Thank You! In Jesus' name I pray. Amen.

The Pain of Consequences

Read Genesis 3:1–24

Key Verse:

*So the Lord God sent him out from the garden of Eden,
to work the ground from which he was taken.*
GENESIS 3:23 NLV

Understand:

- *There are natural consequences to your
sins. God allows them because He will
use them to teach you a better way. He
never wastes any opportunity to instill a
life lesson. It's how He helps you become
more like Jesus. Have you seen this truth
in your life?*

- *Remember that even though man was
separated from a life with God in
paradise, when you accept Jesus as your
Savior that separation is over and you're
now connected to God forever. Have you
asked Jesus to be Lord of your life?*

Apply:

Their life changed that day. Adam and Eve directly
disobeyed God, giving in to lies from the enemy. In
his crafty way, he made them doubt God's goodness.

He made Eve feel she was missing out on something. He swayed them into violating the one rule God set for them in the Garden. And the consequences were brutal.

Some people believe God is mean. But the truth is that He doesn't want you to ruin your life or do things that will make you unhappy. God created commands to keep you safe. They are in place because He loves you! At times, it may be hard to embrace them because they feel stuffy or restricting, but you can trust that God has them in place for your protection.

Where are you struggling to make the right choice? What makes it challenging to follow God no matter what? Ask Him for strength and wisdom to follow Him even when disobeying feels easier and more fun.

Pray:

God, help me see that Your commands are there to help me avoid brutal consequences. And when I do make the wrong choices, thank You that You will always make everything work for good in my life. I know perfection isn't Your goal, but I need Your help to live with purpose. In Jesus' name I pray. Amen.

The Trap of Lying

Read Genesis 4:1–15

Key Verse:

But afterwards the Lord asked Cain, "Where is your brother? Where is Abel?" "How should I know?" Cain retorted. "Am I supposed to keep track of him wherever he goes?"
GENESIS 4:9 TLB

Understand:

- *You may be able to get away with lies here on earth, but they will not be hidden from your Father in heaven. And chances are your dishonesty will eventually catch up with you and result in painful consequences. Have you seen this play out in your life?*
- *The truth is that we all mess up. We're not perfect. And it's important to remember that you can make it right by taking responsibility and asking for forgiveness. It will go a long way. Are you in the habit of confessing your sins to others and God?*

Apply:

Cain thought he could get away with murder. When he planned it out in his head, it must have left him with a false sense of security that he would get away with it. But soon after, God confronted him. And when God asked Cain about his brother, He already knew what had been done. Cain miscalculated his plan and his God.

It's easy to lie, especially when you think doing so will save you from getting caught. The problem is that developing that habit and lying on the regular becomes a way of life. Dishonesty loses its conviction and you lie without worrying about consequences.

Sure, there are little white lies that don't seem to really matter, but they matter to God. And the more you get comfortable with those, the easier it is to move on to the bigger lies.

Choose to be an honest young woman. Be a champion for truth.

Pray:

God, I know truth matters to You. Give me the courage to be honest even when I know it could land me in trouble. I don't want to get comfortable with being dishonest because it will eventually end in painful consequences. Even more, it's not Your plan for my life. Help me be strong. In Jesus' name I pray. Amen.

Do It Anyway

Read Genesis 6:8–22

Key Verse:

Noah did everything God commanded him to do.
GENESIS 6:22 MSG

Understand:

- *God sometimes asks things of you that others may consider silly or ridiculous. He may ask you to stand out morally, choosing a different path than your friends. And God may ask something of you that feels scary and overwhelming. What might keep you from saying yes? And how can you overcome it?*

- *Consider the privilege of being commissioned by God. Of all of the people in the world, He chose you for the job. And because He did, that means He will equip you for the task. How does that settle in your heart today?*

Apply:

What a sad state of the world for God to be so frustrated that His plan for redemption was to destroy every living thing on it. In all the earth, Noah was the only person who pleased Him. This righteous man stood his moral ground even though everyone else—literally every other human being—was ruled by their sinful nature.

Do you think today's society is that different from in Noah's time? It doesn't take a rocket scientist to see the mess we are in morally. But that only sets that stage for you to shine God even brighter into the darkness of the world. It shouldn't depress you. Instead, it should make you more resolved to be a modern-day Noah who lives according to God's beautiful plan.

It may not be the popular way to live, but do it anyway. Not because you are better than others but because you know that it matters to God.

Pray:

God, I want my words and actions to be a light for others so they can see You. Give me the grit to make the hard, moral choices. Give me the guts to stand up for what I know is right. And give me the wisdom to know when to do both. No matter the pull of the world to be self-seeking, I want to do the right things. . . anyway. In Jesus' name I pray. Amen.

Built for Community

Read Genesis 11:1–9

Key Verse:

*"Come, let us go down and give them
different languages, so that they won't
understand each other's words!"*
GENESIS 11:7 TLB

Understand:

- *Think about how easy it is to hang out
  with people who think the same way you
  do. It's comfortable and safe. But God
  may be wanting you to branch out with
  friendships. Is there someone He's put on
  your heart lately?*

- *God built you to be in community. He's
  for it! But sometimes friends in your
  group start down a path of bad choices
  and you're faced with a decision. Do you
  stay or do you find a new group? Make
  sure you don't compromise because it's
  easier than making new friends.*

Apply:

God's command was simple: Go all over the earth and multiply. The flood was over, and it was time to repopulate the world with new life. But instead of obeying His command, the group wanted to stay together.

We like our people, don't we? We have our besties whom we could never imagine being without. And while God created you for that kind of community, sometimes His plan is for you to move on.

There are friendships that may last a lifetime and others that are seasonal. Your job is to listen to God's voice so you can be where He wants you to be. Community changes when you move states or schools. It can look different when you change teams or summer jobs. Friendships can shift when you start choosing opposite activities or interests. And as much as you may want to hold on, ask God to show you His will for that relationship.

Pray:

God, it's hard to imagine letting go of some of my friends. I know it may be for the best, but would You please speak loudly enough that I can hear Your will over mine? I want to hold on to the right friends and not cling to the ones I need to release. Give me the ears to hear You clearly. In Jesus' name I pray. Amen.

Don't Hide Who You Really Are

Read Genesis 12:1–20

Key Verse:

*"Please say that you're my sister. Then everything will
be alright for me, and because of you I will live."*
GENESIS 12:13 GW

Understand:

- *Surround yourself with people who think
  that who you are is enough. Be wise in
  who you befriend and who you date,
  because too often people try to change
  others into someone else. Do you believe
  God created you perfect in His sight?*
- *When God made you, He wasn't in a bad
  mood. You weren't an afterthought or an
  inconvenience. God took His sweet time
  making you into the amazing person you
  are today. What three things do you love
  most about yourself? Tell them to God.*

Apply:

Abram was afraid for his life and less concerned for
his wife. In that moment, he was more worried about
surviving than making sure his marriage was thriv-
ing. In his fear, he asked his wife to be someone she

was not. How do you think that made her feel?

Can you think of someone who told you that you were not okay? Has there been a voice in your life that's been a constant reminder that you needed to change to be loved or to be accepted? Sweet one, that is not how God feels about you.

You delight your heavenly Father—stumbles, fumbles, and all. He made you on purpose and with purpose, and His heart for you is so very good. Trust that you were an intentional creation, especially when someone tells you the opposite. And if you need reminding, ask God to make it so.

Pray:

God, sometimes it's difficult to believe that I am good enough. The world's voice is very loud, and I hear the negative messages all the time. It's hard to not want to change so I can fit in or be loved. Would You help me be strong enough to remember who I am and Whose I am? I am thankful for how You've made me. In Jesus' name I pray. Amen.

Fight for Those You Love

Read Genesis 14:1–16

Key Verse:

As soon as Abram heard that his nephew had been taken prisoner, he gathered a company of his most reliable and best-trained men (there were 318 of them, all born in his household) and pursued the enemy as far north as Dan.
GENESIS 14:14 VOICE

Understand:

- *You're surrounded by some amazing family and friends. When hard times hit, one of the kindest things you can do is be there to help. Consider being a shoulder to cry on, an ear to listen, or feet to walk it out with those you love.*
- *It's hard to stand in the middle of someone's mess with them. It takes compassion and perseverance. Think about how much it meant when that person loved you through a rough patch. What can you do now for someone who needs an ally in their battle?*

Apply:

Did you notice that *as soon as* Abram heard that his nephew was in trouble, he acted? He didn't ignore it. He didn't put it at the end of his to-do list, or think his time was too valuable or that he had better things to do. Instead, Abram immediately gathered his finest men and went after Lot.

Investing in the lives of others is messy business. But God created you to be in community with others. He knows we each need a tribe of people to come alongside us as we walk out our one and only life. And so often He uses others to be His hands and feet, helping one another through tough times.

Who needs you right now? Who is God putting on your heart to help? Go fight for them. And if you ask, God will give you exactly what you need to do it.

Pray:

God, help me be the kind of girl that is always willing to help others. I want to be someone others can depend on when they are struggling. I want to be unafraid to get messy with those I love. Give me courage and strength and endurance. In Jesus' name I pray. Amen.

The Choice to Believe

Read Genesis 15:1–21

Key Verse:

*Then Abram believed in the Lord,
and that made him right with God.*
GENESIS 15:6 NLV

Understand:

- *Think about how much faith it takes to believe something you feel God has laid on your heart. Think of how doubt begins to creep in. Think about how fear makes it hard to allow yourself to get excited. So, how do you hold on to God's promise?*
- *Life is a series of choices—some easy and some hard. How does insecurity wreak havoc on your ability to be confident in your choices? Who is someone you've seen trust God no matter what? This week, reach out and ask them for encouragement.*

Apply:

Abram had to make a choice. Would he choose to believe what God told him, even though it must have seemed almost impossible? Or would Abram let that nasty seed of doubt keep him from trusting God's promise? He chose to believe, and it made him right with God.

You live in a world so full of broken promises it's almost impossible to believe what you're told, isn't it? Keeping your word isn't a high priority in today's society, and it has taught us that vows are easily broken and unreliable.

But that's not God's way. When He promises something, He never takes it back. He will not let you down. He won't forget about you. God intends to make good on His promise in His perfect time. And when you decide to hold on to that vow no matter what, it deeply delights His heart because He knows the effort it takes.

Pray:

God, I want to be right with You. I want to delight Your heart with my choice to believe You. Give me the kind of faith it takes to trust You in all things. In Jesus' name I pray. Amen.

Stay or Away: What's the Best Choice?

Read Genesis 16:1–16

Key Verse:

"You decide," said Abram. "Your maid is your business."
Sarai was abusive to Hagar and Hagar ran away.
Genesis 16:6 msg

Understand:

- *Think about how you usually respond to hard situations. Do you stand up and advocate for yourself, or do you run away in an effort to avoid confrontation? Is your usual response the best choice?*
- *Sometimes staying and fighting for what's right is the right thing to do. But other times, the smart choice is to walk away. It's not that you're a coward. It's that you have wisdom to know what's best. Can you remember seeing this play out in your life or someone else's?*

Apply:

Hagar had it rough. She was put in a lose-lose situation and punished for carrying a child she never wanted to carry. While she may not have had the best attitude, it was no excuse for abuse. It never is.

And feeling overwhelmed by all she was enduring, she chose to run away because it seemed the best choice. There was no way for her to win.

Maybe you are feeling the same as Hagar—unloved, unappreciated, unseen. Maybe there are haters in your life who make it almost unbearable to get through the day. Maybe your family is in a tight spot and everyone's bad mood seems to be pointed in your direction. Maybe a friend turned her back on you and is sharing secrets you never meant to be shared.

You have a choice to make. Do you stay and advocate for yourself, or do you walk away in wisdom? This is a God-sized question, friend. What does He have to say?

Pray:

God, I don't always know the right way to respond. And standing up for myself feels so much scarier than walking away. I need to know Your will for me in these situations. I want to do what's right. Please show me what that is. In Jesus' name I pray. Amen.

God of the Impossible

Read Genesis 17:1–27

Key Verse:

*Abraham fell flat on his face. And then he laughed,
thinking, "Can a hundred-year-old man father a son?
And can Sarah, at ninety years, have a baby?"*
GENESIS 17:17 MSG

Understand:

- *How do you respond to situations that
  look impossible? Do you throw your
  hands in the air and walk away in
  defeat, or do you accept the challenge and
  look for solutions?*
- *It's vital to remember that God is God
  and you are not. There are times you
  can find answers in your own strength,
  but there are other times you have to
  completely rely on God for them. How do
  you know the difference?*

Apply:

God had just revealed His epic plan for Abraham
and his descendants. In that moment, He made a
covenant, promising things to him only God could
make possible. Abraham was intrigued, excited, and

probably in complete awe. And then God shared a promise that made Abraham fall down and laugh. The idea of him fathering a child at the ripe old age of 100 felt impossible. But not to God.

How about you? Has God whispered things that feel overwhelming and unrealistic? Maybe it's to speak up or speak out about hard things. Maybe He's promised something that doesn't seem possible because of bad choices you've made. Or maybe you feel unqualified to follow the path He has laid out for you.

Let God be God. He specializes in the impossible. He can do anything, fix anything, change anything. Your job is to be obedient to do the next right thing.

Pray:

God, life feels so impossible sometimes. And I often feel unqualified to move forward in the things You're asking me to do. They scare me. Would You remind me that You are the God of impossible things and that my job is to trust You? In Jesus' name I pray. Amen.

Longing for the Wrong Things

Read Genesis 19:12–29

Key Verse:

But Lot's wife, from behind him, [foolishly, longingly] looked [back toward Sodom in an act of disobedience], and she became a pillar of salt.
GENESIS 19:26 AMP

Understand:

- *Think about the things you miss—the items, places, or relationships you don't have anymore. Are any of them better left in the past? Is that season of life gone for a reason? Take time to journal your thoughts.*
- *Have you considered that longing for things God has removed from your life is an act of disobedience? Maybe even foolish? How do you know when something should be left in the past and when it's worth fighting for?*

Apply:

And just like that, she turned into a pillar of salt. Many argue that looking back was her way of innocently remembering what she was leaving behind.

But God was clear in His directive to not turn around. Their life in the city of Sodom was nothing to miss. He was saving them, and turning back toward the city was disobedience.

Part of trusting God is trusting His reasoning. You don't always get to know the *why*—at least not this side of heaven. He says in His Word that His plans for you are always good plans. So when God is clear, telling you what to do or what not to do, you can (and you should) confidently trust Him.

God's heart for you is always good!

What is God asking you to leave behind? What makes doing so difficult? And how can you choose faith over your fleshly desires so you can stay in God's will?

Pray:

God, sometimes Your will for my life makes no sense. It's confusing. But I am choosing to trust that Your reasons are right and Your heart for me is good. Help me remember this when I am confused. In Jesus' name I pray. Amen.

What's First in Your Life?

Read Genesis 22:1–18

Key Verse:

"Lay down the knife; don't hurt the lad in any way," the Angel said, "for I know that God is first in your life—you have not withheld even your beloved son from me."

GENESIS 22:12 TLB

Understand:

- *Is God first in your life? If others were to see how you live your life and the choices you make, would they agree that God is first? What do your actions and words reveal as the most important?*
- *Sometimes God asks very hard things of you—things that pull you so far out of your comfort zone. Maybe it was speaking up or stepping away. Maybe it was letting go or holding on. How did you respond?*

Apply:

God asked Abraham to do something unbelievably difficult. He asked him to sacrifice the child God had promised to him and Sarah. Isaac was a miracle baby on so many levels, and it's not hard to imagine the gut-punch such a request would pack. But because God was first in Abraham's life, this man of God stepped out in obedience without question.

Think about it for a second. Where does your relationship with God rank in your life? When you consider friends and school, family and sports, and everything in between, where does God fit in? Does He get your attention every day or is He easily replaceable? Do you think God feels like a high priority on your calendar?

Take inventory of your priorities and find ways to connect with God in meaningful ways every day. It matters. How can you make Him feel first in your life?

Pray:

God, I'm sorry for not putting You first. Life gets so busy and it's easy to let things slip—even the things I really care about. I'm committed to putting You first. You are important to me! Remind me to spend time with You when I forget. We're in this together, right? In Jesus' name I pray. Amen.

You Be You, Let Them Be Them

Read Genesis 27:1–35

Key Verse:

Look, my brother Esau is a hairy man,
and I have smooth skin.
GENESIS 27:11 VOICE

Understand:

- *Consider the pressure to fit into the box society has created. Every day, you face the stress of trying to fit in rather than being yourself. Where do you feel the burden of being different than how God created you? Where does it come from?*
- *What messages are you listening to right now? Are you surrounded by people who celebrate who you are, or do you keep company with those who encourage you to be a different version of yourself? What changes do you need to make?*

Apply:

Rebekah's decision to make Jacob pretend to be his brother showed a lack of judgment. The message was simple: if you change your appearance, there's a reward on the other side. So Jacob listened to his mother and presented himself as Esau, but it cost him something.

Have you ever thought that if you were different—thinner, smarter, stronger, funnier—you'd be better? Maybe you'd be more popular or be noticed by the cute boys. Maybe you'd get the academic award or be the lead in the musical. Maybe somewhere along the way, you decided who you are right now wasn't enough. So instead of embracing your awesomeness, you created a fake version of yourself, hoping for acceptance.

God made you on purpose. All your quirks and uniqueness. All your nerdiness and coolness. They were all intentional. So be yourself. If God wanted you to be different, you would be. Even more, He delights in you!

Pray:

God, I want to feel confident in who You made me to be rather than try to be someone else. I don't want to always look for the approval of others because I know it's a dead-end street. Will You remind me that I was created to stand out. . .to be different? And give me the courage to walk that out every day. In Jesus' name I pray. Amen.

Hard Work Pays Off

Read Genesis 29:15–30

Key Verse:

So Jacob worked seven years for Rachel. It was only like a few days to him, because of his love for her.
GENESIS 29:20 NLV

Understand:

- *Have you ever worked hard for something—poured out your blood, sweat, and tears for it—and rather than feel drained or overwhelmed, the time spent was a joy? It didn't leave you stressed or wear you out emotionally. What made it different from other kinds of work?*
- *Working hard because of the end reward makes sense because you know what's coming and decide it's worth your time and toil. But how can you be joyful even if the outcome isn't glamorous or is unknown?*

Apply:

Rather than receive Rachel's hand in marriage after seven years of work, Jacob ended up with her younger sister, Leah. The story is full of twists and turns, but Jacob had to work another seven years to earn Rachel's hand. He had to be joyful and focused rather than frustrated and flippant.

It's easy to finish the project when you know the teacher will give you a good grade, and easy to run miles at practice knowing you'll start the game. But it takes grit and integrity to give your best when you're not sure your efforts will pay off.

God created you to work. There are things He knew only you could do because of the awesomeness inside you. So when you whine and complain or give anything less than your best effort, you're missing out. Even more, those around you won't get the benefit from what you can bring to the situation or project.

Pray:

God, help me be a hard worker in all things. I know my determination will pay off in the end, benefitting me and those involved. I want to be joyful and full of integrity in the work I do—be it at school, at home, on a team, or at my job. I know it matters! In Jesus' name I pray. Amen.

Be the Voice of Reason

Read Genesis 37:1–36

Key Verse:

"Let's not have any bloodshed. Put him into that cistern that's out in the desert, but don't hurt him." Reuben wanted to rescue Joseph from them and bring him back to his father.
GENESIS 37:22 GW

Understand:

- *Have you ever lied to cover something up? Or maybe you didn't speak up when you knew others were heading down the wrong path? What role does the Holy Spirit's voice play in your life when you're faced with tough choices?*
- *Have you ever considered that you have the ability and privilege to influence those around you? Have you ever considered yourself a role model? What keeps you from being a voice of reason to those you hang out with?*

Apply:

Joseph's brothers were so jealous of him. In frustration, they plotted his demise. But Reuben tried to be the voice of reason. Unfortunately, his best efforts failed and his brothers didn't listen.

Your job is not to make others do the right thing. Honestly, you don't have that kind of power over anyone. You can't force others to listen to your wisdom, but you can stand up for what you know is right and speak truth to your friends and family anyway.

God has given you the ability to know right from wrong. And His Holy Spirit in you will guide you as you make choices. It may be scary to stand up and speak out when you feel prompted. Sometimes being the voice of reason isn't popular. But have you considered that maybe God put you in that very situation, with those friends, because He wanted you to help them make the right decision?

Pray:

God, I want to be a voice of reason. I want to be known as someone who lives her life faithfully, not perfectly. Would You help me know when I need to speak up? Would Your Holy Spirit nudge me when I need to speak out? I want to be a good friend and a loving family member who loves others well. In Jesus' name I pray. Amen.

You Make a Difference

Read Genesis 39:1–23

Key Verse:

It happened that from the time that he made Joseph overseer in his house and [put him in charge] over all that he owned, that the LORD blessed the Egyptian's house because of Joseph; so the LORD's blessing was on everything that Potiphar owned, in the house and in the field.
GENESIS 39:5 AMP

Understand:

- *As a Jesus girl, you bring Him into every situation and relationship because the Holy Spirit lives in you. That means you make a difference by just being there. How does this challenge you?*
- *Think about ways you can bless others with your presence. Does a friend need you to sit with her through a tough conversation? Is there someone who could use a friendly face? Remember it's God in you that brings blessings to those around you. It's His presence working through you that encourages others. Who can you comfort right now?*

Apply:

Did you notice that the Lord blessed *because of* Joseph? God's favor was on him, and Potiphar's home benefitted while Joseph worked there. Even when thrown into jail, the Lord's favor was on Joseph and the warden trusted his leadership. Everywhere he went, God was with him and it made a difference.

God's presence is with you too. Be it your classroom, club meeting, team practice, band concert, job, or the place you volunteer, your presence blesses others because of God in you.

It's not about your pride, it's about your faith. When you spend time in the Word and in prayer, when you trust God and follow His path for you, your faith becomes strong. And because you're willing to let God be God, you give Him room to mold you into a beautiful Jesus girl. You become wise, compassionate, and courageous. . .and that blesses others.

Pray:

God, I want to make a difference in the lives of those around me. I want them to see You through me. Grow me into the young woman You want me to be so I can be a strong witness for Your power and glory. In Jesus' name I pray. Amen.

The Big Picture
Read Genesis 45:1–28

Key Verse:

*"Now do not be distressed or angry with yourselves
because you sold me here, for God sent me ahead
of you to save life and preserve our family."*
GENESIS 45:5 AMP

Understand:

- *It's hard to see the big picture when you're
  in the middle of the mess. The middle
  is where the situation looks bleak and
  hopeless. But what if you trusted that
  God isn't done yet? What if you decided to
  believe that He will give you perspective
  in due time?*
- *You don't always get the inside scoop on
  what God's doing. You have to trust God
  each step of the way. How can you be an
  encouraging voice when someone you love
  is struggling with a hard situation?*

Apply:

Joseph's perspective was on point. Seeing his brothers again opened his eyes. He wasn't bitter they'd
disliked him nor angry they'd sold him. Joseph didn't

blame them. Instead, God blessed him with the big picture.

It's easy to get stuck in situations that often feel unbearable. You're distraught for being dumped by that guy or cut from the team. You're frustrated for not getting the lead in the musical or that summer job. And sometimes, it's easy to get mad at God because you've prayed for these things and they still didn't happen.

But what if you decided to trust that God is in control, and if He wanted you to date the boy, make the team, get the lead, or be hired for that job. . .it would've happened? What if you asked God for the big-picture perspective, thanking Him for always knowing what's best?

Pray:

God, help me trust that You see the big picture and know all things. Help me realize that You are in control and have the best planned for me. Help me believe that Your plans for me are good, always on time, and exactly what I need. In Jesus' name I pray. Amen.

Burning Bush Moments

Read Exodus 3:1–22

Key Verse:

God saw that he had stopped to look. God called to him from out of the bush, "Moses! Moses!" He said, "Yes? I'm right here!"
EXODUS 3:4 MSG

Understand:

- *Moses wasn't seeking God when He spoke to him, but He definitely got his attention. Think about the ways God gets your attention. How does He speak to you?*
- *There are some people who don't believe God is alive and active today. They don't think He speaks or performs miracles anymore. Journal about the times you felt God leading you in a certain direction, and thank Him for being present in your life.*

Apply:

Do you ever pray, asking God to put a huge lighted billboard in your path to show you the way to go? Sometimes we all want His answers to be obnoxiously evident because we're confused on what's the next right step for us. And because we don't want to miss it, we cry out for our own burning bush moment.

The truth is that God doesn't hide the path He's chosen for you. While He may not reveal every detail, He will always show you the next right step. The Word clearly says that if you seek Him, you will find Him. He doesn't play mind games or give you confusing hints to decode. He simply says that when you need answers. . .ask. He will make them recognizable.

It's okay, however, to remind God that Moses needed a big sign. It's okay to ask God to make His answers to your prayers super obvious. He loves you and created you to be in a relationship with Him. That means when you talk to your Father in heaven, He's deeply delighted! So friend, where do you need His help right now?

Pray:

God, I need a burning bush moment. I'm confused and afraid to take the wrong turn. But even if I hear You wrong, I know You will reroute me. You want the best for me, and You'll honor my pursuit for the right path. In Jesus' name I pray. Amen.

When You Feel Unqualified

Read Exodus 4:1–17

Key Verse:

But Moses said to the LORD, "My Lord, I've never been able to speak well, not yesterday, not the day before, and certainly not now since you've been talking to your servant. I have a slow mouth and a thick tongue."
EXODUS 4:10 CEB

Understand:

- *Moses—one of the greatest leaders in history—struggled to feel qualified. Can you relate to his response to God? Have you ever felt like you didn't have what it would take to do what God is asking? How does this story of Moses encourage you?*
- *There are a million excuses we use to say no to God. What are the ones you use? And what would happen if you decided to say yes instead?*

Apply:

Feeling unqualified is something everyone struggles with from time to time. You're not alone if you lack the confidence and courage to follow God's leading in your life. It often takes His supernatural strength to be able to trust enough to say *yes*. Maybe God included stories like Moses' to remind you that He didn't make a mistake commissioning you for the job.

Remember that God doesn't call the qualified . . .He qualifies the called. In other words, if He chooses you for the task, God will give you what you need to walk it out. That doesn't mean it will be easy (or horrible, either). But it's assurance that you will have the tools and skills and wisdom when you need them.

Where is God asking you to step out in faith? Where is He asking you to have epic courage? What situations are requiring you to trust Him more than your circumstances?

Pray:

God, I don't feel right for the job. It feels too big and scary and overwhelming, and I'm going to need you to give me the boldness to say yes. I want to be willing to follow You no matter what, but I need You to please fill me with strength and bravery. In Jesus' name I pray. Amen.

You Can't Control Others

Read Exodus 5:17–6:9

Key Verse:

Moses reported this to the Israelites.
But they would not listen to him because they were
so discouraged by their back-breaking work.
EXODUS 6:9 GW

Understand:

- *It can be so frustrating when others*
  ignore you. Maybe you have information
  that could help them avoid a heartache
  or offer a different perspective on the
  situation. How do you respond when
  people don't listen?
- *You can't control others. You can't make*
  them hear you or do what you ask. We're
  each given a free will to make our own
  choices—good or bad, right or wrong. All
  you can do is share what God has laid on
  your heart. How does this free you?

Apply:

The Israelites were understandably cranky. They'd
been in slavery for so long. And when Moses told
Pharaoh to free them, his request instead made

conditions tougher. In their eyes, this man sent to end their bondage didn't make things better; he made them worse. No wonder they didn't want to listen to what he had to say.

Remember, Moses wasn't there to win a popularity contest or shame others into listening to him. God didn't send him to make sure he was heard and believed. Instead, his only job was to speak on behalf of God and then watch Him soften or harden their hearts into action or inaction. Moses didn't have the power to control their responses. His job was to speak.

Release yourself from the expectation that you're doing God's job. Instead, choose to share truths laid on your heart and trust God to do the rest.

Pray:

God, thank You that I'm not responsible for making people obey. That's a heavy burden that weighs me down. I know that sometimes Your only expectation of me is to use my words to encourage or suggest, leaving everything else to You. Help me remember that. In Jesus' name I pray. Amen.

Protect Yourself from Evil

Read Exodus 12:1–31

Key Verse:

The blood on the doorframes of your houses will be a sign of where you are. When I pass by and see the blood, I will pass over you. This plague will not afflict you when I strike the land of Egypt with death.
EXODUS 12:13 VOICE

Understand:

- *The world is full of opportunities for bad things to creep into your life. There are negative influences you have to choose to ignore every day. What are some practical ways to protect yourself so you don't open the door to them?*

- *Because God is all-knowing, we can be certain that He knew what homes belonged to the Israelites, yet He asked them to mark their doorframes anyway. Why do you think He required their participation when He could have handled it all on His own?*

Apply:

The death of the firstborn was the final plague set to sweep through the land of Egypt. Moses and Aaron had followed God's orders, asking Pharaoh to free the Israelites. But up to now the royal had snubbed his nose at their request despite all the chaos God had brought their way.

In the previous plagues, God had spared the Israelites from them all. In this final one, however, God required their participation.

What a great reminder that sometimes God keeps you tucked away from evil. You may not even know all He has saved you from. But there are other times God asks you to make a choice. He is expecting you to protect yourself from bad influences, dangerous situations, blatant sin, and beliefs that don't align with Truth.

Where is God asking you to stand your ground? What is He asking you to protect yourself from? Where is He requiring your participation?

Pray:

God, show me the situations and people that I need to be aware of. I want to make good choices so that I will live in Your peace rather than in chaos. Will You give me wisdom and discernment to see those moments clearly? And will You give me the courage to take action? In Jesus' name I pray. Amen.

The Power of Remembering
Read Exodus 13:1–22

Key Verse:

*"Tell your child on that day: 'This is because
of what GOD did for me when
I came out of Egypt.'"*
EXODUS 13:8 MSG

Understand:

- *Think back to stories your parents or
  grandparents told you about things your
  family has been through in the past.
  What was the theme of their stories?
  What did you love about them?*
- *It's important that we remember special
  moments because they serve purpose. They
  can inspire, protect, connect, and support.
  Consider starting a journal of all the
  moments you want to remember.*

Apply:

The Israelites knew they had to remember the
goodness of God so they could pass that truth on to
their children and generations to come. They knew
the power of sharing their experiences with family
and communities. And since they didn't have books

or iPhones to store those stories, they relied on word-of-mouth.

Your story is your testimony. All those times God showed up in your life can serve as powerful encouragement to others going through a hard time. They are reminders to hope and trust when things look bad. Can you remember a time someone's story gave you the courage to not give up? Or when knowing someone made it through a similar situation as the one you're in helped to build your confidence?

We all need to remember that God is our helper, provider, and deliverer. We need to remember that He will protect and heal us. Those are powerful truths to cling to when we need them the most.

Pray:

God, I know that our testimonies are powerful because they often make us brave. It's so good for my heart to remember all the ways You've showed up for me and for others I care about. When I'm discouraged or when a friend needs encouragement, remind me to think back to all the times You were there in mighty ways. You're so awesome. . .all the time. In Jesus' name I pray. Amen.

Waiting and Watching for God

Read Exodus 14:13–31

Key Verse:

"The LORD will fight for you while you [only need to] keep silent and remain calm."
EXODUS 14:14 AMP

Understand:

- *Sometimes it's so hard to keep silent and remain calm when you hit rocky times. What do you think is the benefit of responding this way? What usually happens when you don't?*
- *What does it mean when someone says the Lord will "fight" for you? What has that looked like before and/or what might that look like next time? Is it hard to trust that He will show up? Why or why not?*

Apply:

This verse is often a hard one to walk out, wouldn't you agree? It's not easy to keep your mouth shut when you feel wronged. And staying calm may even be harder. When someone hurts you, lashing out in anger is a more natural reaction to the hurt you're feeling. But God says to let Him handle it.

If you're quick to defend yourself or have the last word, you've taken that initial opportunity away from God to fight for you. And chances are, your quick reaction only added fuel to the fire anyway.

What would it take for you to step back and let God battle instead? According to Moses, it would take calmness and quietness. This isn't taking away your voice or suggesting what you think and feel doesn't matter. Tell God everything—get all the hurt and anger out—and then watch and wait as He fights for you.

Pray:

God, help me give You room to work in my life. I need a huge dose of calm and quiet so I'm not constantly fighting for myself. I know You'll do a better job anyway. Help me know the battles I'm supposed to fight and the ones You are. And give me the confidence to trust You. In Jesus' name I pray. Amen.

Don't Complain. . . Trust

Read Exodus 16:1–18

Key Verse:

The Israelites said to them, "If only we had died by the LORD's hand in Egypt! There we sat around pots of meat and ate all the food we wanted, but you have brought us out into this desert to starve this entire assembly to death."
EXODUS 16:3 NIV

Understand:

- *Are you a complainer? Do you focus on all you don't have rather than what you do have? What keeps you from being content? How would your life be better if you were satisfied rather than always hungry for more?*
- *Think about people in your life who are drama queens. They tend to overreact and exaggerate, throwing a bit of a temper tantrum along the way. What kind of payoff do they get for acting that way? How does it improve or hurt their relationships?*

Apply:

The Israelites were quick to forget the miracles, signs, and wonders they'd just witnessed at the hands of God. They saw over and over as God took care of their every need. They watched as Pharaoh finally released them from slavery. They saw the sea part as they walked the dry ground to the other side. They watched Him meet their every need. They saw it all yet found reason to complain anyway.

Have you ever forgotten the times God showed up for you? Do you sometimes worry if He'll fix that relationship, bring new friends, heal the disease, give you courage, help you forgive, or show you the answer? And does that worry ever come out as anger with a hint of drama?

The next time you want to complain instead of trust, take a breath. Then remind yourself of the times God has been there for you, and thank Him.

Pray:

God, I can be quick to forget all the ways You've taken care of me and instead grumble in my frustration. Help my unbelief in You! I know You are my provider in all ways, and I'm so grateful. Would You give me a long memory of Your goodness in my life? In Jesus' name I pray. Amen.

Built for Community

Read Exodus 17:8–16

Key Verse:

But Moses' hands grew tired. So they took a stone and put it under Moses so he could sit down on it. Aaron and Hur held up his hands, one on each side of him so that his hands remained steady until sunset.
EXODUS 17:12 CEB

Understand:

- *God created you to live in community. You need friends to help you navigate the ups and downs of life. Think of all the ways friendships have blessed you. How does your friendship bless them?*
- *Have you ever thought about how important it is to stand by your family and friends while they're battling tough situations? They need encouragement and support for those times they get tired or scared or want to give up. Who might need your help right now?*

Apply:

What a beautiful picture of friends helping friends. All the pressure for the win was on Moses and his ability to keep his arms raised in the air. Held high, the army was winning. But when his arms began to lower from exhaustion, the opposing army had the upper hand. Thankfully, Hur and Aaron stood on either side of Moses and held up his arms when he couldn't any longer.

Aren't you glad God knew how much we needed friends? Think through your last week and those times a friend said kind words, bought you ice cream, helped you process hurtful words, gave you a ride, let you borrow a favorite shirt, or invited you to her party. Those friends are gifts from God, here to bless you.

Are you being a good friend back? Are you available to support others when they need help? Remember, God has blessed others with your friendship too.

Pray:

God, thank You for friends! I'm thankful You created us to be in community because together is so much better than alone. Help me choose my friends wisely, and help me be a positive force in their lives too. In Jesus' name I pray. Amen.

What Do You Worship?

Read Exodus 20:1–26

Key Verse:

No other gods, only me.
EXODUS 20:3 MSG

Understand:

- *What are the things you worship? God is clear there's to be nothing above Him, but sometimes we forget how easy it is to put other things first. Today, think about what gets the majority of your time, money, and attention. Then see where God fits in.*
- *You may live a busy life between school, extracurricular activities, family time, friend time, work, and volunteering. What are some practical ways you can spend time with God throughout your day?*

Apply:

God doesn't mince words when He says there should be *no other gods*. He rightly deserves your devotion and praise. And while you may not worship other gods like Buddha or Allah, it's easier than you might think to place everyday things and much-loved people above Him.

Who or what gets your time? Netflix? Friends? Music? Working out? Parties? Books? Sports or theater? Work? When you let any of these things become more important than God, you're actually putting them higher on your priority list than Him. They become godlike because you focus your time on them more than anything else. And too often, that means God gets what's left over.

Make sure that you find ways to connect with God throughout your day. Talk to Him about what frustrates you. Thank Him for helping and guiding you. Tell Him you love and appreciate who He is in your life. Share your hurt feelings and hopeful expectations. And when you do, you're actively letting God know there is no other god above Him.

Pray:

God, You are the most important part of my day. Forgive me for not always showing You that, and help me be more mindful that I don't let anything or anyone take Your place. Please bring reminders into my day to connect with You. You are so very worthy of my time and attention! In Jesus' name I pray. Amen.

The Problem with Impatience

Read Exodus 32:1–24

Key Verse:

When the people realized that Moses was taking forever in coming down off the mountain, they rallied around Aaron and said, "Do something. Make gods for us who will lead us. That Moses, the man who got us out of Egypt—who knows what's happened to him?"
EXODUS 32:1 MSG

Understand:

- *Are you a patient person? Think about how you feel when you have to wait in line for your favorite ride or wait for a table at your favorite restaurant when you're starving. How does waiting affect your attitude and choices?*
- *This is a microwave society where people want things to happen immediately. Patience isn't a strong suit for many. What is the value in learning to be patient? What are the consequences if you're not?*

Apply:

Moses took a little more time on the mountain than the Israelites thought was necessary, leaving them aggravated. Instead of trusting their leader and their God, they became annoyed and irritated. They got bored. And scripture tells us they complained to Aaron and talked him into making a *replacement* god.

How many times have you found yourself over-anxious as you wait for God to show up? Especially when desperate, it's normal to want to grab the reins of control or put your trust in something or someone else. But too often your desire for instant answers leads to unhealthy alternatives that leave you empty.

What's the hardest part about waiting on God? Do you worry He'll forget to respond or not show up altogether? Ask God to grow your trust of Him so you can be patient as you wait for His help. Learn to let God be God, having faith in His timing and His will for your life.

Pray:

God, I need Your help as I learn to trust You more and better. I struggle with patience and need an increase in faith so I can wait confidently in You. In Jesus' name I pray. Amen.

Not without God

Read Exodus 33:1–17

Key Verse:

For Moses had said, "If you aren't going with us,
don't let us move a step from this place."
Exodus 33:15 TLB

Understand:

- *What would it look like for you to live*
  your life refusing to move forward
  without God's presence? How would that
  affect your decisions? How would that
  affect your relationships? How would
  it affect your everyday life?
- *What might it mean to the heart of God*
  to know you desire a relationship with
  Him above all else? Moses told God he
  didn't want to be anywhere God wasn't.
  Can you relate? How might you shift
  your perspective or schedule to develop
  that same mind-set?

Apply:

Every day you get to choose whether you include
God in your day or not. You get to decide if you go it
alone or if you invite God to journey with you. Will

you ask for His guidance or find your own wisdom? Will you depend on the advice of friends or ask God for His discernment?

Moses put his foot down about traveling without God because he knew the value of walking with Him. He knew that all wisdom comes from Him, and he needed it for the task ahead! And Moses trusted God to lead and provide for his every need.

What about you? God is available twenty-four hours a day, seven days a week, three hundred and sixty-five days a year. You have access to His strength, power, peace, discernment, and courage anytime you need it. Decide now that walking through your day without His presence isn't acceptable. Then invite God into your day, from the moment you awake until you close your eyes at night.

Pray:

God, You are a good Father, and I need Your guidance and companionship every day. I don't want to be where You are not. Thank You for being accessible anytime I need Your help. In Jesus' name I pray. Amen.

God Chose Them for You

Read Deuteronomy 5:1–21

Key Verse:

"Honor (respect, obey, care for) your father and your mother, as the Lord your God has commanded you, so that your days [on the earth] may be prolonged and so that it may go well with you in the land which the Lord your God gives you."
DEUTERONOMY 5:16 AMP

Understand:

- *Think about what God is asking in the verse above. In what ways can you honor, respect, obey, and care for your parents? This must be very important to God because He included it in the Ten Commandments.*
- *Even when it doesn't feel like it, God handpicked your parents for you. Whether they're the ones you were born to, the ones who adopted or fostered you, or are your stepparents, they were chosen specifically for you. How does that make you feel?*

Apply:

You may think your parents are irrelevant, annoying, overbearing, or just plain weird, but God gave you to them on purpose. Of all parents to live on planet earth—past, present, or future—the Lord chose them. It may be normal to feel like they're unrelatable, but it's important to know that God's plan is intentional.

What if you chose to honor that truth? On those days they make you angry, overreact to a situation, say the wrong thing, or ask more of you than you think is fair, what if you made a choice to honor God's decision. You may pray, *"God, I'm not a fan of my parents right now, but I trust You so please help me respect them."*

Scripture says that when you choose to honor, respect, obey, and care for your mom and dad, it will make your life a better one. And who doesn't want that?

Pray:

God, it's not always easy to love my parents, but I know
You want me to. Would You help me remember that
I can trust Your decision to put them in my life,
and that You'll give me the ability to honor and
respect them? Help me love them the best
I can. In Jesus' name I pray. Amen.

Are You All-In?

Read Deuteronomy 6:1–19

Key Verse:

Love the LORD your God with all your heart,
all your being, and all your strength.
DEUTERONOMY 6:5 CEB

Understand:

- *In your opinion, what does it mean to love God with all your heart, all your being, and all of your strength? Think of ways you are already doing this, and also think of ways you could be doing this better. Spend time today telling God your thoughts about and struggles with this command.*

- *What scares you about choosing to be all-in with God? Have you been hurt by someone in the past and it's made you scared to love someone again? Do you struggle to trust God because of it? Ask God for revelation and healing today.*

Apply:

Think about what it means to love with all of your heart. . .to love God with all of your being. . .and to love Him with every bit of strength you have. It may be easier to replace the word *all* with the words *some* or *most*, because *all* is a tall order. It requires everything you've got, and that's hard to give.

Why do you think God commands so much from you? Why doesn't He want to settle for a piece of your heart, a smidge of your being, and a little bit of your strength? Maybe it's because He designed you and knows the beauty of what you have to offer. Maybe it's because God created you to be in community with Him. Or maybe it's a mixture of both.

The One who knows you inside and out wants to be at the top of your list of priorities. He wants you to be all-in.

Pray:

God, I want to be all-in. I want to put You above all else and love You with everything I am and everything I have. You, Lord, are worth every bit of my time and my energy. Help me love You well! In Jesus' name I pray. Amen.

Keeping Him in the Mix

Read Deuteronomy 8:1–20

Key Verse:

*Don't think to yourself, My own strength and
abilities have produced all this prosperity for me.*
DEUTERONOMY 8:17 CEB

Understand:

- *Think back over the past few weeks.
  Where have you seen God show up
  in your life? What good things have
  happened that can only be attributed to
  His faithfulness?*
- *Does your desire for God slack when life
  is good? And does it pick back up when
  things get tough? How do you think He
  feels about that? What needs to change?*

Apply:

Moses wanted to make sure the Israelites remem-
bered the faithfulness of God. He knew their
tendency would be to look at their comfortable,
prosperous lives and pat themselves on the back.
God had showed up countless times for His chosen
people, proved Himself trustworthy in every way,
and Moses wanted to make sure they gave credit

where credit was due.

Think about your life for a minute. It's easy to cry out to God when you're struggling in a friendship, worried about a grade, or concerned that your parents are fighting too much. It's in those times we crave God's presence more than ever.

But when everything is going as planned, so often we become distant from God because we don't feel desperate for His help. Even more, we start to credit ourselves for all the good happening, certain it's because of our awesomeness alone. And while our hard work does pay off, our source for strength, wisdom, perseverance, and courage comes from God.

Simply put, you can do what you do because of His love and support.

Pray:

God, I need You every day. Forgive me for the times I don't keep You in the mix and instead go it alone. I want You in the good and bad, and I will try to remember that all that I am and all that I can do is because of You. In Jesus' name I pray. Amen.

The Call to Be Brave

Read Deuteronomy 34:5–Joshua 1:9

Key Verse:

"Haven't I commanded you? Strength! Courage!
Don't be timid; don't get discouraged. GOD,
your God, is with you every step you take."
JOSHUA 1:9 MSG

Understand:

- *Being afraid is a normal, human response. It's just a reality we all face. So think about what scares you the most right now. Then as you reread the verse above, how do God's words make you feel about these fears?*
- *What does courage look like to you? How have you seen God increase your ability to be brave in the past? Where do you need Him to do that right now?*

Apply:

Just like Joshua, we also need reminders to be brave and courageous in the things we face. Sometimes we think about the hard conversation we need to have, the friendship we need to let go, the pile of home-work to complete, or the tryout we're about to do, and we let fear get the best of us. Instead of being courageous, we give in to our doubts and anxieties.

The key to facing those fears is remembering that God is with you. For every step you take forward, He is there offering you His strength and His courage to walk out those hard moments. You don't have to navigate those times alone. Friend, you are never alone.

Being afraid may be part of the human condition, but that doesn't mean you can't be brave. Sometimes it means you do the scary things anyway. You trust God scared, believing that He will give you courage when you need it the most.

Pray:

God, thank You for promising to never leave me, especially in those fearful moments. I know that fear may be part of life, but it's what I choose to do with that fear that matters. I want to be brave, Lord. And with Your help, I can be. Help me remember that so I can be courageous enough to take the next step. In Jesus' name I pray. Amen.

Why We Need to Remember

Read Joshua 4:1–24

Key Verse:

"You should answer, 'The water of the Jordan River was cut off in front of the ark of the LORD's promise. When the ark crossed the Jordan, the river stopped flowing. These stones are a permanent reminder for the people of Israel.'"
JOSHUA 4:7 GW

Understand:

- *It's easy to forget the times and ways God showed up for you. But it's the testimony of His faithfulness that gives hope for the difficult situations you'll face. Take some time today to remember God's goodness.*
- *What visual can you create in your room as a reminder of all God has done? Is it words in a journal? Stickers on your mirror? Rocks in a jar? Consider creating a visual reminder of times God intervened in your life.*

Apply:

The reason we need to remember God's faithfulness is for those moments we freak out about a situation.

Sometimes we just need visual reminders that God has shown up because it builds our faith that He'll do it again. And so often, that truth is something we're desperate for.

When the Israelites crossed the Jordan River—at flood stage and on dry ground—it was one more instance they saw God's hand on their life. By this time, they'd witnessed countless miracles and wonders and *still* needed reminders that God was invested in their life.

Friend, we do too. When it all hits the fan (and it will hit the fan) we need to know that God is there and He sees us. Even more, we need to know that He'll help us get to the other side of our own Jordan River.

There is power in remembering God's faithfulness. How can you make sure you do?

Pray:

God, thank You for wanting to be part of my life. Thank You for all the times You showed up for me. Help me find a very personal way I can memorialize those moments so they will encourage my heart in the future. You are so good to me, and I love You so much. In Jesus' name I pray. Amen.

Do It Anyway

Read Joshua 6:1–20

Key Verse:

So the troops shouted very loudly when they heard the blast of the rams' horns, and the wall collapsed. The troops charged straight ahead and captured the city.
JOSHUA 6:20 GW

Understand:

- *Trusting God sounds easy but is often hard to walk out. Where is He asking you to have faith in His plans and ways right now?*
- *Consider the truth that God's thoughts are not your thoughts and His plans are not the same as yours. How is this a good thing? Why should this make you rejoice with gladness?*

Apply:

What a wonky battle plan to take the city of Jericho. Walk around the city, toot horns, and scream. There's no doubt many of the Israelites thought this plan to be silly. Maybe some wondered if Joshua had heard God correctly. But Joshua didn't hesitate. He trusted God and His plan and carried it out regardless of how silly he might have looked to others.

That is epic faith!

Maybe God is asking you to trust Him and it doesn't make sense. Maybe your prayer request is being answered in a crazy way. Maybe God is being silent when He usually isn't. It's hard to have faith when things don't look like they normally do or when you're forced to step out of your comfort zone.

Resolve to trust Him in the predictable and the unexpected. Choose to take that step of faith even when it doesn't necessarily make sense. Decide to do it anyway.

Pray:

God, help me trust You no matter what. It's not my place to question You. Instead, it's my privilege to place my full faith in You. I know that Your heart for me is good and that Your plans are for me to prosper. Thank You for loving me so well! In Jesus' name I pray. Amen.

Go Ahead, Ask for the Impossible

Read Joshua 10:1–14

Key Verse:

There had never been such a day before, and there has never been another since, when the Lord stopped the sun and moon—all because of the prayer of one man. But the Lord was fighting for Israel.
JOSHUA 10:14 TLB

Understand:

- *What keeps you from asking bold prayers? Is it insecurity? Are you afraid He will be angry? Think of one "impossible" situation you're currently facing and ask God for what you want, and for the understanding if He answers another way.*
- *Think about how this moment in Joshua's life encourages you. Why do you think God chose to include it in His Word? What does He want you to learn from it?*

Apply:

Can you even imagine a crazier request than for the sun to literally stop in the sky? Joshua knew he needed the sunlight so he could defeat his enemies, and so he boldly asked the Lord to stop the earth from rotating on its axis.

Joshua wasn't afraid to ask for something that seemed impossible. Are you? Where do you need God's help but are afraid to ask for it? Do you think God is incapable or unwilling?

Maybe your parents are divorcing and you want them to reconcile. Maybe a cross-country move is planned but you want to stay put. Maybe you want to be friends with a certain group of girls but can't find a way to connect.

Sweet one, be bold like Joshua in your requests to God. He may not always say yes, but He will also listen and answer in the way that's best for you.

Pray:

God, I love that I can come to You and ask for things that feel impossible. Thank You for being approachable about anything and everything. Give me the confidence to be bold in my requests. In Jesus' name I pray. Amen.

God-Given Girl Power

Read Judges 4:1–24

Key Verse:

When Sisera had fallen sound asleep from exhaustion, Jael, Heber's wife, took a tent peg and walked quietly toward him with a hammer in her hand. She hammered the tent peg through his temples into the ground. So Sisera died.
JUDGES 4:21 GW

Understand:

- *Do you ever feel that you're less than because you are a girl? Do you think it makes you a second-class citizen? Read back through chapter 4 in Judges and notice how God trusts Deborah and Jael. What stands out?*
- *God empowers women of all ages to do incredible things. Think of times in your life when you've seen examples of strong women. What did they have in common? How do they encourage you right now?*

Apply:

Jael killed a man in such a gory way. The details of that story may be hard to stomach, but like Deborah in that same chapter, she chose to obey God. The point of the story isn't that murdering is acceptable. It is not. But the point is that God often chooses women for hard tasks. He values everyone equally, and in His mind and heart girls are just as awesome as boys.

Maybe God included their stories in His Word so that you would know that you have immeasurable value to the One who created you. God doesn't measure worth by your sex, skin color, age, or anything else. Instead, He is looking for the faithful ones willing to step up and step out for Him.

Warrior, God equipped you with a huge dose of girl power, and He is hoping you will choose to use it to further the kingdom.

Pray:

God, thank You for creating me to be strong in You. Thank You for valuing girls just as much as boys. And thank You for empowering us to be warriors for Your kingdom. Help me stand in my God-given girl power every day! In Jesus' name I pray. Amen.

The Lies We Believe

Read Judges 6:11–24

Key Verse:

But, Lord, how am I supposed to deliver Israel?
My family is the weakest in the tribe of Manasseh,
and I am the least of my family.
JUDGES 6:15 VOICE

Understand:

- *What do you think about yourself? Do you see the good things, or do you only focus on things you don't like? Why?*
- *Are you believing lies about yourself? When someone says you're not good enough, too much or too little, less than lovable, or something else hurtful. . .do you automatically believe them? Gideon thought little of himself, but God saw him quite differently and chose him for a huge task. How does this encourage you?*

Apply:

Every day you're bombarded with lies—hurtful untruths about who you are. From rude comments, to perfect images on social media, to high expectations from others, to your own bullying thoughts, it's easy to let truth become clouded by lies. Every day you have a choice to make: will you adopt those lies as your truth, or will you believe you are who God says you are?

You may ask, *what does God really think about me?* That's a fair question and an important one. Because if you're to choose to believe Him over the lies, you have to know that His heart for you is good, right?

That's where God's Word comes into play in your life. In its pages, God talks to you. It's where He reveals who He is and where He reminds you who you were created to be. The Bible is a powerful weapon to help battle hurtful lies. Make time to read it every single day.

Pray:

God, like Gideon, I sometimes get confused about who I am. I feel weak, inadequate, or unworthy. Regardless of what others say of me, I want to have courage to stand firm in the truth of who You made me to be. Help me ignore the lies and embrace Your truth. In Jesus' name I pray. Amen.

Be Trustworthy

Read Judges 16:4–22

Key Verse:

So he told her his whole secret. He said to her,
"No razor has ever touched my head, because I've
been a nazirite for God from the time I was born.
If my head is shaved, my strength will leave me,
and I'll become weak. I'll be like every other person."
JUDGES 16:17 CEB

Understand:

- *Are you a trustworthy friend? Being a safe place for those you care about is so important. Who are the family members and friends you can trust with your heart?*
- *While keeping secrets for others is important, sometimes it's in the best interest to tell a trusted adult what's going on because your friend's safety is at risk. Think about what kind of secrets told to you would warrant sharing with an adult.*

Apply:

Delilah was digging for information to hurt Samson. She may have acted like she cared for him, but she didn't. She made a deal with the Philistines, agreeing to exchange Samson's secret for a bunch of silver. And once he shared that confidential information with her, it was the beginning of the end for Samson.

When someone chooses to open up to you, it's important you choose to be a trustworthy friend. Maybe your friend is struggling with their parents' divorce and wants to talk, is being left out of the group and feels unwanted, or needs advice on how to handle a rude teammate. If they are willing to open up, decide to be a safe friend.

Can you identify the loyal and faithful friends in your life? And can you also identify those who are not? Be smart with your heart, and be reliable to those who share theirs with you.

Pray:

God, I want to be a faithful friend. I want to be trustworthy for those I care about. But I also want to know when to involve a trusted adult so my friend stays safe. Will You give me discernment and wisdom to know the difference? In Jesus' name I pray. Amen.

Choose to Be Loyal and Faithful

Read Ruth 1:1–22

Key Verse:

But Ruth said, "Do not urge me to leave you or to turn back from following you; for where you go, I will go, and where you lodge, I will lodge. Your people will be my people, and your God, my God."

RUTH 1:16 AMP

Understand:

- *Think about what Ruth was giving up to stay with her mother-in-law. She was young and could remarry but chose instead to keep company with Naomi. What stuck out to you in this story?*
- *Being loyal is a powerful way to tell someone they matter to you and is a key ingredient to a good relationship. Who are your faithful friends? How can you let them know how much their friendship means to you?*

Apply:

Ruth was a rock star. When she decided to stay with Naomi, she knew it could end her chances to remarry and have a family. But love for her mother-in-law trumped her own desires. More than anything else, Ruth wanted to be loyal and faithful to Naomi.

It's hard to look past our own desires and focus instead on someone else's. Because our default button is to look out for number one, choosing to put someone's needs ahead of our own is a big deal. Even more, God sees and will bless it.

As Ruth's story goes on, she ends up meeting Boaz, getting married, and having a son named Obed. He later became King David's grandfather, placing Ruth in the direct lineage of Jesus.

God saw and blessed Ruth's loyalty. And sweet girl, He will also bless you for being selfless and faithful to those you love.

Pray:

*God, give me the heart to choose the needs of others ahead of mine. I know my needs matter and I'm not supposed to be a doormat, so help me know when to be selfless and when to take care of myself. Sometimes those lines are blurry. I want to be loyal and faithful to the people You put in my life. Help me be.
In Jesus' name I pray. Amen.*

Choosing to Be Kind

Read 1 Samuel 1:1–28

Key Verse:

*But her rival wife taunted her cruelly,
rubbing it in and never letting her forget
that GOD had not given her children.*
1 SAMUEL 1:6 MSG

Understand:

- *Why do you think certain people choose to be mean toward others? Why do you think they enjoy making someone feel bad? Have you ever? If so, what was your motivation?*
- *If God commands us to love others, how can we justify treating anyone cruelly? Even when they hurt you or say ugly things, you don't have to respond likewise. How can you treat others with respect and protect yourself at the same time?*

Apply:

Sometimes choosing to be kind to others is challenging, especially when they're not kind to us. It's a choice we have to make every day and in every situation we face. We can be nice or we can be mean.

The choice is ours.

God wants you to be kind. That doesn't mean you're a doormat that everyone gets to walk all over. That doesn't mean you have to let others bully or make fun of you. And it certainly doesn't mean you are weak or unworthy of love.

It just means that you take your faith seriously.

It means you're choosing not to treat them the way they've treated you.

And instead of stooping to their level, ask a trusted adult for help and ask God for wisdom. Advocating for yourself is a powerful skill. It's choosing to be kind to yourself.

Pray:

God, I don't want to be bullied nor do I want to be the bully. Help me choose kindness every time. I know it won't be easy, but I trust that You will give me the strength and courage to be that kind of girl. I want to be a safe place for my friends and family. In Jesus' name I pray. Amen.

Don't Be Afraid to Follow God

Read 1 Samuel 10:1–27

Key Verse:

So they inquired further of the LORD, "Has the man come here yet?" And the LORD answered, "He is there, hiding himself by the provisions and supplies."
1 SAMUEL 10:22 AMP

Understand:

- *God rarely asks His followers to do easy things. To do what He is asking often requires big faith and boatloads of trust. Can you remember a time you obeyed God even though it was super hard? What was the result?*

- *Did you notice that God knew Saul was hiding? As a matter of fact, He is the one who pointed it out! Are you ever tempted to hide from doing what's right or what you believe God is asking of you? Why or why not?*

Apply:

Saul was hiding. It's funny to think this soon-to-be-named king was so scared of stepping into his God-given role that he tried to hide. The truth is that walking out God's will can be scary and hard and make us feel insecure in our abilities. Have you ever experienced that in life?

Maybe you felt nudged to share Jesus with a friend or share your testimony at youth group. Maybe you felt led to go on the mission trip rather than the summer camp with friends. Or maybe you felt God asking you to tithe to church instead of buying new clothes. Sometimes we get scared about what He may be asking or feel inadequate for the job, and so like Saul. . .we try to hide instead of embrace what we believe God is asking.

Think about those fears that keep you stuck, unwilling or unable to follow God's leading. What are you afraid of? Have you told God about it?

Pray:

God, I don't want to be scared to follow Your plans. Even when it feels too big or too overwhelming, help me trust You enough to say yes to the plans You have for me. I know You love me and are trustworthy. Thank You for that! I love You too! In Jesus' name I pray. Amen.

The Constant Bully

Read 1 Samuel 17:1–25

Key Verse:

*Each morning and evening for 40 days,
the Philistine came forward and made his challenge.*
1 SAMUEL 17:16 GW

Understand:

- *We each have giants we have to face, and
  many of them stick around and taunt
  us on the regular. What are some of the
  giants you're facing today? How do you
  respond to them?*

Apply:

The Philistine was a giant named Goliath, and he was an epic fighter with huge muscles, proper training, and top-of-the-line weapons. There is no doubt he was a force to be reckoned with. And every day for forty days, he stood before the Israelite army, bullying them with his words. King Saul and his men were scared because they forgot how powerful their God was.

You have bullies too—situations and people that freak you out. It could be a health concern or a rude teammate. You may bully yourself with thoughts of inadequacy about the big class presentation in a few weeks. Maybe there are mean girls who are making your school year miserable. Yes, we will all face giants in our lives, which is why we can't forget that our powerful and faithful Father is stronger!

Never forget He is always with you and always for you. And when you need His help, ask Him to defeat the giants that constantly taunt you.

Pray:

God, sometimes the giants in my life really scare me. They just feel too big to handle on my own. Thank You for being a protective Father, and help me remember to ask for Your help when I feel overwhelmed. There are no giants You cannot defeat! In Jesus' name I pray. Amen.

Courageous Faith

Read 1 Samuel 17:26–58

Key Verse:

*"Today the LORD will hand you over to me. I will
strike you down and cut off your head. And this day
I will give the dead bodies of the Philistine army
to the birds and the wild animals. The whole
world will know that Israel has a God."*

1 SAMUEL 17:46 GW

Understand:

- *Think about how much faith it takes to
  trust that God will give you what you
  need when you need it. It's risky to trust
  like that, but can you remember the times
  you took the risk? What were the results?*
- *What do the words "courageous faith"
  mean to you? Can you think of Bible
  characters, family members, or friends
  who live out this kind of faith? What do
  you notice about their life that encourages
  you?*

Apply:

David had no room for doubt. Rather than worry, he
held steadfast to his courageous faith. In his bones he

knew that God would equip him to defeat Goliath. And so David stepped in and stepped up, and the rest is history.

Where do you need that kind of faith today? What situation or person is challenging you to flex your faith muscle like never before? What circumstances are causing you to be fearful or insecure?

Are you worried a friendship might be over? Are you concerned about a struggle within the family? Are you trying something new or giving up something that you've loved? Are you switching teams or friend groups? Do you feel inadequate for the job you're about to start or unprepared for the semester?

Your courageous faith in God will give you the strength, wisdom, and perseverance you'll need to battle any giant that comes your way!

Pray:

God, help me not live in doubt and worry. I want to be a bold believer, certain that You will give me everything I need to face the hard things in life. And in those times I feel weak and unable, remind me that You are always with me, no matter what. In Jesus' name I pray. Amen.

The Urge to Cover it Up

Read 2 Samuel 11:1–27

Key Verse:

He wrote in the letter, "Place Uriah at the front of the fiercest battle, and then pull back from him so that he will be struck down and die."
2 SAMUEL 11:15 CEB

Understand:

- *When you make a mistake or willfully do something wrong, do you ever try to cover it up? God isn't expecting perfection from you. What keeps you from owning up to your misjudgment?*
- *How would this world be different if everyone chose to be honest? What would it look like if people took responsibility for their blunders and bloopers? Consider modeling this to your friends and family.*

Apply:

David made a horrible error in judgment. Not only did he have relations with a woman married to another man, but he then had her husband killed so the truth was kept hidden. Even more, with Uriah out of the picture David could marry Bathsheba.

This king was a hot mess of bad decisions. He could have owned his bad choice and asked for forgiveness. He could have repented and made things right. But David decided the best plan was to cover up his sin.

Maybe you can understand his choice to hide what he'd done. Chances are, you have too.

Sometimes it feels safer to keep our blunders and bloopers hidden so we don't have to walk out the consequences. But God knows everything. And He is ready and willing to forgive your every sin when you confess them to Him.

It's always best to just be honest. No one thinks you're perfect, but you can choose to be honest.

Pray:

God, help me be the kind of girl who isn't afraid to own my mistakes. I know there may still be consequences, but You will reward honesty. Every time I consider a cover-up, would You please remind me of that truth? In Jesus' name I pray. Amen.

Drawing a Line in the Sand

Read 2 Samuel 18:1–18

Key Verse:

*The man told Joab, "Even if I were to feel the weight of
a thousand pieces of silver in my hands, I would not put
out my hand against the king's son; for we all heard
the king command you, Abishai, and Ittai, saying,
'Protect the young man Absalom, for my sake.'"*
2 SAMUEL 18:12 AMP

Understand:

- *In your opinion, what's the difference
  between setting boundaries and building
  walls?*
- *Consider the value of setting up
  boundaries now so you don't have to
  make those hard choices in the heat of the
  moment. What are some decisions you can
  firm up today with regard to your morals,
  your relationships, your faith, and peer
  pressure?*

Apply:

This unnamed man drew a line in the sand. He
decided to obey King David's command to protect
his son, Absalom. And no matter the temptation to

cross the line—even for a ton of silver—he'd set a boundary he was unwilling to compromise.

There will always be lures and cravings that will try to persuade you to cross the lines you've set for yourself. It's hard to stay true to what you know is right because society often has different standards than those of Jesus. What they say is true and right rarely aligns with what the Bible says. And even more, the pressure to fit in often requires you to cross the boundaries you've put in place.

Ask God to help you stand firm against temptations. Ask Him for the courage to stand your ground even when it may be the unpopular decision. Ask for wisdom and discernment to see when you're getting too close to the line you've drawn in the sand.

Pray:

God, I want to be the kind of girl that sets healthy boundaries and doesn't give in to peer pressure. I don't want to compromise the moral and relational boundaries that glorify You and benefit me. Help me be strong enough and wise enough to weather those temptations with confidence. In Jesus' name I pray. Amen.

Who Is God to You?

Read 2 Samuel 22:1–51

Key Verse:

*He is my True God, my stronghold in whom
I take refuge, My strong shield, my horn that calls
forth rescue, my tall-walled tower and strong
refuge, My savior from violence.*

2 SAMUEL 22:3 VOICE

Understand:

- *Who is the one you trust to help you
  navigate tough situations? What is it
  about them that makes you trust their
  help?*
- *Think about how you view God. Is
  He helpful and loving? Is He angry,
  withholding His favor? Is He available
  to you, or do you think God is too busy?
  How does your view of Him affect your
  relationship with Him?*

Apply:

To David, God was his everything. He was true, a
stronghold, a place for refuge, a shield, a rescuer, a
tower, and his savior from trouble. This king knew
His only hope was in the hands of God, and so he

decided to trust and believe that the Lord would be who he needed Him to be.

Who is God to you?

Think back to times you've seen Him show up. What were the results? Did He heal you or someone you loved? Did He make a way when it looked like there was no way out? Did God open a door at the right time or did He close one to protect you? Did He give you courage, wisdom, strength, peace, or perspective when you had none?

David was in the habit of telling God what he thought of Him. It probably encouraged him to remember and delighted God to hear. Spend time telling God exactly who He is to you.

Pray:

God, thank You for being such an amazing God. I'm thankful You love me so deeply and are invested in every part of my every day. Please give me the eyes and ears to know You are working in my life, especially when I feel alone and scared. I need You. In Jesus' name I pray. Amen.

Where True Discernment Comes From

Read 1 Kings 3:1–15

Key Verse:

"So give your servant a discerning heart to govern your people and to distinguish between right and wrong. For who is able to govern this great people of yours?"
1 Kings 3:9 niv

Understand:

- *Have you ever asked God for discernment? Have you asked Him to show you right from wrong in a situation that's confusing? If no, what keeps you from it? If so, how did it help you navigate those circumstances?*
- *If you don't know what discernment means, take a moment to look it up. How does it differ from wisdom? Why is it important to have both?*

Apply:

We all need good judgment so we can live our best life. We need to be able to see right from wrong, looking past the obvious and into a deeper understanding of the situation. Being a Jesus girl means we choose to live with strong morals and character that reflect the Lord's heart.

And honestly, this is almost impossible without God's help.

We're limited by our human condition. We aren't anywhere close to perfect, and even our best-laid plans to live right can take a sharp left turn into bad decisions and choices—often before we even realize it. Our heart may be in the right place, but even then, we don't always have the ability to make the best judgment call.

But you know what? God promises to give you discernment when you need it. It's something you can ask Him for every single day. It is a heavenly gift that allows you to see the details of a challenging situation clearly, and helps you determine the right next step.

Pray:

God, please give me a discerning heart. I want to be able to see the right path from the wrong one. I want to recognize good from not-so-good in my everyday life because I want to glorify Your name with my choices. In Jesus' name I pray. Amen.

The Power of Prayer

Read Ezra 9:1–15

Key Verse:

At the evening sacrifice I got up from my misery, and with my clothes torn, I knelt down, stretched out my hands to the LORD my God in prayer.
EZRA 9:5 GW

Understand:

- *Have you ever been in a situation that felt too big or too confusing, and the only option you had was to pray? What was the end result? Peace? Wisdom? Hope? Something else?*
- *What are your thoughts on prayer? What does it look like in your life? Do you think there is a right way or a wrong way to pray? Does your family pray? What does it mean to you?*

Apply:

Ezra prayed a desperate prayer that day. He knew God's people had messed up again, and he wanted to help make things right. Ezra knew this was something only God could fix, and so he cried out for His forgiveness and help.

What an awesome example. This prophet reminds you that so often God is your only hope. And while it's easy to try to remedy the situation yourself, inviting God into the mix is a smart move because He has the power to make things right again.

Whether it's a friendship struggle, a family feud, a class schedule, a team dynamic, a work issue, a hard confession, or anything else you face in life. . .there's power in prayer because God is on the other side of it listening to everything and already making a way for you.

Talk to God and invite Him into your situation. Thank Him, confess, and ask for what you need. He's all ears.

Pray:

God, thank You that I can share my life with You through prayer! I'm so grateful that You're always available to me, and You are interested in everything going on. Help me remember to include You in the good and hard times. I think You're awesome. In Jesus' name I pray. Amen.

Armed and Ready

Read Nehemiah 4:1–23

Key Verse:

Those who carried materials did their work with one hand and held a weapon in the other.
NEHEMIAH 4:17 NIV

Understand:

- *Think about scriptures that comfort you when life gets hard. Consider keeping a journal in your purse or backpack with these verses so you can access them when you need encouragement.*
- *Who are the secret weapons in your arsenal? What friends and family are always willing to listen, offer sound advice, and walk the hard path with you? This week, think of ways you can thank them for being a powerful weapon against the enemy's plans.*

Apply:

The opposition was so great against Nehemiah and the Israelites. They were committed to restoring the wall surrounding Jerusalem, but their enemies had every intention to shut the project down. Instead of giving in to fear, Nehemiah told them to work with one hand and hold a weapon with the other.

This is great advice. The truth is that the enemy of your soul wants to stop you from walking out the plan God has for you and your life. He wants to intimidate you, scare you, and overwhelm you. But you get to choose if his tactics work or not.

There are plenty of weapons available to you, like God's Word, prayer, and community. All of these things can help you stay the course, empowering and encouraging you to keep moving forward.

Whenever God builds, the enemy tries to destroy. Expect opposition when you say yes to God, but don't give in to it. Grab your weapons and do the next right thing.

Pray:

God, it's so frustrating that the enemy wants to ruin everything You're doing in my life, but I am not a wimp. Because of You, I am a warrior with an arsenal of weapons at my disposal to keep me focused and motivated. Thank You for knowing I'd need them. You think of everything. In Jesus' name I pray. Amen.

You Are More Than Your Looks

Read Esther 1:1–22

Key Verse:

Bring Queen Vashti to my party! Tell her to put on her royal crown and to wear her finest clothes. I want to show off her beauty in front of my distinguished guests.
ESTHER 1:11 VOICE

Understand:

- *What kind of pressure do you feel to be beautiful? Do you put pressure on yourself to look a certain way? Do your friends or boyfriend have those kinds of expectations? How does that make you feel?*
- *God is the One who created you. He chose the way you would look and decided the details of your appearance, and God doesn't make trash. Do you struggle with this truth? Why or why not?*

Apply:

The queen refused to go before the king and his guests. She knew they'd been partying, and showing up felt vulnerable. She may have been tired of people only noticing her looks without seeing the depth of her heart. Vashti may have been scared for her safety, not sure what her husband would have required of her.

So rather than risk it, she said. . .no.

The world may tell you that it's all about how you look. It may place importance on your body instead of your brains. Society may say you have to possess beauty to be loved or accepted.

But that is not what God says.

Sweet one, don't believe the lie that you're deemed valuable based on your looks. Everyone is beautiful in their own way—inside and outside. And never forget that your immeasurable value comes from being a daughter of the Most High King. . . alone.

Pray:

God, it's hard to live in a world that makes beauty the most important thing. Sometimes I struggle to feel accepted because of that. Will You remind me that You made me in Your image and that You delight in me— just the way I am? In Jesus' name I pray. Amen.

Your Protective Daddy

Read Psalm 17:1–15

Key Verse:

*Protect me from harm; keep an eye on me like you
would a child reflected in the twinkling of your eye.
Yes, hide me within the shelter of your embrace,
under your outstretched wings.*
PSALM 17:8 TPT

Understand:

- *Think about your earthly father. Is he the
  kind of dad that considers you the apple of
  his eye? Does he protect you?*
- *Chances are your earthly father has fallen
  short a time or two. He is human and
  flawed, just like you. Ask God to help you
  extend him grace, and for the heart to
  love him as he is. God chose him for you
  on purpose.*

Apply:

Your heavenly Daddy is terribly protective of you.
Anything that comes into your life—the good
and the not-so-good—has received His stamp of
approval and is only allowed if it will benefit you and
glorify Him. He is crazy about you, a proud Father!

God wants only the very best for His daughter.

So knowing all that, think about the fact that He is the One who chose your earthly father. How does that make you feel? Because the truth is that sometimes these men are the bomb-diggity, and other times these men fall very short of awesome. Sometimes they make us feel loved and special and other times not so much.

Regardless of the flaws of your earthly dad, your heavenly One will never let you down. He will never turn His back. He will never hurt you. And even more, God will give you the grace and perspective to love your here-and-now dad even in his imperfection.

Pray:

God, thank You for being the perfect dad. Thank You for loving me perfectly and knowing every detail of my life. And thank You for my earthly father. Help me love him through thick and thin, trusting that You put us together on purpose. In Jesus' name I pray. Amen.

Those Dark Days
Read Psalm 23:1–6

Key Verse:

Lord, even when your path takes me through the valley of deepest darkness, fear will never conquer me, for you already have! You remain close to me and lead me through it all the way. Your authority is my strength and my peace. The comfort of your love takes away my fear. I'll never be lonely, for you are near.
PSALM 23:4 TPT

Understand:

- *You're never promised an easy life. Nowhere in the Bible does it say that you'll be free from hard times. So when the struggles come, how do you respond? Do you buckle up and hold on to God, or do you freak out?*
- *Think of the times when you felt God the closest. What was going on in your life? How much were you investing in your relationship with God?*

Apply:

This verse is one of the most quoted because it helps us find strength that God is there and we will be okay. The reality is that we will have those dark days whether we want them or not. And it's this reminder that helps us stay strong and trust God through them.

Are you there now?

Are you battling fear over a friendship, feeling abandoned or rejected? Maybe the class or job ended up being harder than expected and you're facing some potentially difficult consequences. Maybe there's a health concern for you or your parents are considering a divorce. Those are the kind of things that force us to walk through the valley of deepest darkness.

But sweet one, God is right there with you.

He will bring comfort. He will give direction. And He will never leave your side—not for one second. His love will cast out fear and fill you with peace.

Trust Him to walk you through it.

Pray:

God, I'm in a dark place. And it stirs up all kinds of fears of horrible outcomes and endings. Please meet me right in the middle of this mess and help me get through to the other side. I trust You!
In Jesus' name I pray. Amen.

Stop Trying to Be God

Read Psalm 46:1–11

Key Verse:

Surrender your anxiety! Be silent and stop your striving and you will see that I am God. I am the God above all the nations, and I will be exalted throughout the whole earth.
Psalm 46:10 TPT

Understand:

- *Think about how you approach a challenge. Do you work yourself to the bone, trying to make it all come together in your own strength? What do you think the above verse is saying to you?*
- *Do you let God be God? Or do you try to be god by controlling and manipulating situations and people? How would your life look different if you stepped out of the driver's seat?*

Apply:

The psalmist is being very bold, telling us to stop working so hard to make everything okay. We're told to surrender our worries, stop talking about them, refuse to control the situation, and let God work.

That's a tall order! But when we do these things, we'll watch as God brings help and healing where we need it the most.

Where is the hardest place to trust God in your life?

Is it in your plans for the future? Maybe in your fears and anxieties about relationships? Maybe in being willing to forgive someone and move on? Maybe in a tough situation with a parent, coach, boss, or teacher? It's natural to want to try to fix your life yourself. You are very capable! But what if you gave God the reins and let go of the control? What if you decided to let God be God. . .and you be you?

Pray:

God, I'm going to try to let You be in control of my life. I know I need to let go and trust that You will guide me. I know I need to believe that You have my best in mind and will protect me. Give me the courage to step aside and have confidence in You. In Jesus' name I pray. Amen.

You Don't Have to Figure It All Out

Read Proverbs 3:1–35

Key Verse:

Trust GOD from the bottom of your heart; don't try to figure out everything on your own. Listen for God's voice in everything you do, everywhere you go; he's the one who will keep you on track.
PROVERBS 3:5 MSG

Understand:

- *How do you hear God's voice best? As you read His Word? In a sunset? In music? Listening to a certain pastor preaching? What could you change so you could hear His voice better?*
- *Do you really trust God? It may be easy to say "Yes, I do!" but do your actions support your words?*

Apply:

How do you trust God from the *bottom of your heart*? Doing so requires that you choose to believe God is who He says He is and will do what He says He'll do. It's a daily (sometimes hourly) choice to surrender your thoughts, ideas, and plans, making the hard choice to flex your faith muscle.

We're so inclined to try to figure things out on our own. Instead of listening for God's voice, we ask our friends and family for their input. And rather than wait for God to show us the next right step, we follow the path we think is best.

Think about it. What would have to change in your responses to life to make trusting God easier?

Would you have to give yourself a 24-hour time-out before making a move? Ask your friends to pray God will open and close the right doors? Spend time reading the Bible, waiting for Him to speak?

Pray:

God, thank You that I don't have to figure it all out on my own. Life is confusing and hard, and I don't always know the right thing to do. Give me the wisdom to trust You—to listen for Your voice above all the others. More than anyone or anything, I need Your help. In Jesus' name I pray. Amen.

Listen Before You Speak

Read Proverbs 18:1–24

Key Verse:

Listen before you speak, for to speak before you've heard the facts will bring humiliation.
PROVERBS 18:13 TPT

Understand:

- *Listening to others is a gift you give them. Everyone wants to be heard—to be seen. So when you give of your time generously, it blesses others. How can you become a better listener?*
- *Can you remember a time you spoke too soon and made a fool of yourself? When we don't have all the information, we make assumptions that are usually incorrect. Take time to gather all of the details before you make up your mind.*

Apply:

One of the kindest things you can do for those you love is let them have a voice. Allowing your friends space to share how they feel or unpack a bad day tells them you care. It lets them know they're valued. It helps them process life with a trusted friend.

It lets them be heard in a world that is loud and overpowering.

Then once they've been able to talk, ask God for wisdom on how to respond. Do they need advice? Do they need validation? Do they need an apology? Do they need encouragement or perspective? Maybe you need to ask them exactly what they need from you in that moment.

Who are the good listeners in your life? Who are the friends and family who give you room to vent or lament? Who are the safe people who let you open up in honesty and share vulnerably?

Learn from them. Listening is a powerful way to let someone know they matter.

Pray:

God, help me know when to listen and when to speak because sometimes I'm not sure what needs to happen. I want to be wise with my words and wise about when to use them. I want to be a safe place for those I care about. Help me be the best listener I can be. In Jesus' name I pray. Amen.

Anchor Your Hope in God

Read Isaiah 40:12–31

Key Verse:

But those who hope in the LORD will renew their strength; they will fly up on wings like eagles; they will run and not be tired; they will walk and not be weary.
ISAIAH 40:31 CEB

Understand:

- *How do you regroup? When you're tired and weary, what are the things you do to reclaim your energy? Do any of those plans include spending time with God? Why or why not?*
- *Before you walk into a test, have a hard conversation, step onto the field for tryouts, or interview for that job, what if you said a quick prayer asking for confidence? How might that help you in that moment?*

Apply:

We all need hope. It's the most powerful motivator, and without it we fall into deep despair. Hope is what makes us try again or take a risk. It's what gives us the strength to put on our big-girl pants and move forward. Hope is necessary to living with purpose.

God must have known the value of hope, because He established Himself as Hope itself. He promises that if you will have confidence in His power in your life—trusting Him with everything—you will benefit in huge ways! Anchoring your hope in God will give you strength, courage, motivation, and energy to never give up.

Where do you place your hope? Sometimes it's in people or processes. It could be in your own strength or by reading a horoscope. Hope could rest in past successes or a good luck charm. But none of these have the real lasting power to encourage your heart with confidence and bravery. Only faith in God can do that.

Pray:

God, my hope is anchored in You because You're the real deal for true assurance. Remind me that nothing on this earth will satisfy or encourage like You. I'm so glad that You are my God, that You're a safe place, and that You are worthy of my trust. In Jesus' name I pray. Amen.

God Already Knows

Read Jeremiah 29:1–32

Key Verse:

"For I know the plans and thoughts that I have for you," says the Lord, *"plans for peace and well-being and not for disaster, to give you a future and a hope."*
Jeremiah 29:11 amp

Understand:

- *How does it make you feel that God already has complete knowledge of the plans He's made for your life? How does that affect your confidence in Him? How does that affect your ability to trust God?*
- *Have you ever asked God about your future? Have you told Him your hopes and dreams? Take some time this week to talk to Him about it, and then listen to see what He says back to you.*

Apply:

God already knows what's ahead. Before He created you, He thought up detailed plans specific just to you. He determined what was allowed into your life—experiences necessary to grow you to be more like Christ.

We crave to be known. We want to be understood and loved. We want people to see our quirky, crazy, fun-loving, sometimes dramatic sides and accept us.

Well, guess what. God knows you better than anyone, even better than you know yourself. He smiled as He planned you! He put all those facets in you on purpose! And that means you are fully known and fully loved by your Creator.

Even more, He loved you so much that He planned your entire life to be full of hope, peace, and well-being. That doesn't mean things will be easy or perfect, but if you cling to Him. . .you will always get to the other side.

Pray:

God, thank You for knowing me. Thank You for being so intentional in creating me. And thank You for planning out a life full of hope and peace, even though there will be bumps along the way. I know that if I trust You, I'll be okay. In Jesus' name I pray. Amen.

No Matter What

Read Daniel 3:1–30

Key Verse:

"But if he doesn't, you should know, Your Majesty,
we'll never honor your gods or worship
the gold statue that you set up."
DANIEL 3:18 GW

Understand:

- *Think about the faith it took for*
  Shadrach, Meshach, and Abednego to
  make this declaration as they stood in
  front of the furnace. Where do you need
  that kind of resolve in your life right
  now?
- *Are you a bold believer? Do you fully*
  trust God's plan for your life? What
  would need to change to have the kind of
  faith that doesn't doubt God's ability to
  intervene, but will also trust His choice
  not to?

Apply:

These three men are absolute rock stars in the faith.
Talk about raw trust in God! They had no idea if they
would live or die, but they knew without a doubt that

God was full of goodness either way. What a beautiful example of confidence in the Creator.

It's easy to have faith when life is going well. When everything seems to be going your way, trusting God is easy-peasy. But when your foundation is shaken, your security feels threatened, and your future feels unstable, do you still trust Him?

Shadrach, Meshach, and Abednego stood their ground. Will you?

Even when your family is fighting, you're moving across the country, your best friend walks away, you're failing the class, you didn't make the lead in the musical, or you lost a grandparent. . .you can choose to believe God only allowed the hard now because He would somehow use it for your benefit later.

Pray:

God, help me trust Your timing and Your will.
And in those times where You don't do for me what
I really wanted done, please increase my faith to
believe Your heart for me is always good.
In Jesus' name I pray. Amen.

Grateful Gratitude

Read Joel 2:1–27

Key Verse:

*"You will have plenty to eat, until you are full,
and you will praise the name of the LORD
your God, who has worked wonders for you;
never again will my people be shamed."*
JOEL 2:26 NIV

Understand:

- *Where is God meeting your needs right now? Where are you undeniably seeing His hand in your life? Have you thanked Him for it?*
- *How do you praise God? How do you show gratitude to Him? Is it through prayer, singing, journaling, sharing your testimony? What are the best and most natural ways you connect with God?*

Apply:

God takes care of His children. While it may not look or feel like God is in the mix, He promises to always be present and straighten your crooked paths. He'll take care of you and meet every one of your needs. Guaranteed.

Here's where it gets hard to stand firm in your faith. You have to trust that God's way is the best way. You have to trust His timing is perfect. You have to be patient as He works out the details you're not even aware of. You have to have steadfast courage to take the next step and believe God will open and close doors.

And through it all, the challenge is to sit in gratitude, thanking Him every day for working in your life. . .even though you may not see it yet. God is consistently working in your relationships, your maturity, your family, and your everyday activities. And His plans for you are always good.

Pray:

God, thank You for everything. Sometimes I forget that You are my biggest cheerleader and I give credit for good things to myself or to others. Forgive me when I do that! I know that You are my source for everything, and I am so grateful for it all! In Jesus' name I pray. Amen.

Sometimes We Need a Time-Out

Read Jonah 1:1–17

Key Verse:

Now the Lord had arranged for a great fish to swallow Jonah. And Jonah was inside the fish three days and three nights.
JONAH 1:17 TLB

Understand:

- *Sometimes God has to get our attention when we're being disobedient or going down the wrong path. Think of doors that have opened or closed, and ask God for revelation about them.*
- *Has God ever put you in a time-out like He did for Jonah—a period of time where you had space to think or regroup? What did it afford you?*

Apply:

This prophet had a divine time-out. God needed Jonah to take a step back and rethink the path he was on because it was in the opposite direction from God. The Lord had asked him to do something hard—something that scared Jonah—and he tried to hide.

Can we agree that so often the things God asks of us are hard? He wants us to accept an apology from someone who really hurt our feelings, invite the new kid to join the group, say no to a party where we know drinking will take place, or tell the truth when a huge consequence is looming. And if we were honest, we'd admit the option to run and hide sounded much easier.

God loves you so much that He will sometimes put you in a time-out to collect your thoughts. It gives you a chance to think through your choices. And it gives Him time to speak into the situation at hand.

Pray:

God, You think of everything. I'm so glad You use time-outs in my life to get my attention when I'm not making the best choices. More than anything, I want to walk the right path, but sometimes I make the wrong decisions. Thank You for loving me enough to redirect me. In Jesus' name I pray. Amen.

It All Boils Down to This

Read Micah 6:1–16

Key Verse:

But he's already made it plain how to live, what to do, what GOD is looking for in men and women. It's quite simple: Do what is fair and just to your neighbor, be compassionate and loyal in your love, And don't take yourself too seriously—take God seriously.
MICAH 6:8 MSG

Understand:

- *When God asks something of you, He knows good and well that you'll need His help to live it out. He knows your ability requires His help. Do you?*
- *Are you a perfectionist? If you mess up, do you consider yourself a failure? Ask God to free you from it, because it's not His expectation of you.*

Apply:

Have you ever read the CliffsNotes for a book? It boils the big takeaways down into bite-sized morsels. It cuts to the chase, if you will. The verse above is just that. It's a quick reminder of how God wants you to live.

Be fair to those around you. Love others well. Be loyal and kind. And focus on God more than yourself. Through the prophet Micah, God is giving you the CliffsNotes of His overall desire for your life.

Think about these for a moment. Which of them feels difficult to walk out? Are there any that are overwhelming? Do you consider these commands fair or unreasonable? Are you already living this way, or do you have some work to do?

Here is some good truth, sweet one. Every single one of these directives are only possible with God's help. You simply cannot live this way without Him. And even more, He doesn't expect you to perfectly walk these out. But He is looking for you to be purposeful in trying.

Pray:

God, I've got it. Thank You for boiling it down so I know what you're expecting of me. These are things I cannot do on my own, so please help me live out Your commands. I want to follow Your lead and love others well! In Jesus' name I pray. Amen.

God Knows it All

Read Nahum 1:1–15

Key Verse:

The LORD is good, A strength and stronghold in the day of trouble; He knows [He recognizes, cares for, and understands fully] those who take refuge and trust in Him.
NAHUM 1:7 AMP

Understand:

- *What keeps you from reaching out to God when life gets hard? What would need to change for you to trust Him enough with your problems that you share them with Him?*
- *Have you heard the phrase, "You can trust an unknown future to a known God?"*
- *What does it mean to you? How does it connect to today's verse?*

Apply:

Nothing escapes God. He sees every bit of your life lived every day; He has complete understanding of everything you're facing; and He recognizes every time you make the hard choice to put your faith in Him. That means when you decide to trust God with your struggles and challenges, He knows it. And when you run to Him in your hurt or frustration, He realizes your brave choice.

Not only does God recognize your faith and understand the ins and outs of what you're walking through, but He will come to your rescue every time. Through Him, everything you need in that situation or season will be available to you.

Friend, God is a safe place to share the things that beat you down on the regular.

The next time you're in a mess—be it emotionally, physically, or relationally—reach out to God for help and healing. He is good and compassionate, and He will give you strength to get through it.

Pray:

God, You're so awesome. I'm thankful You know me so well. It's a huge relief to know You do, because sometimes I get confused in my hurt and anger. Remind me that You are there for me and to ask for Your help. In Jesus' name I pray. Amen.

This Is Big Faith

Read Habakkuk 3:1–19

Key Verse:

Yet I will [choose to] rejoice in the LORD;
I will [choose to] shout in exultation in the
[victorious] God of my salvation!
HABAKKUK 3:18 AMP

Understand:

- *Every day you have a choice about your faith. You can choose to believe God and trust Him no matter what, or you can let yourself be overwhelmed by the circumstances you're facing. What do you do most often?*
- *Praise is a powerful way to ward off fear. And regardless of the situation, there's always something to be thankful for— even in the yucky seasons or moments. Spend time today recognizing where you've seen God in those times. . .and thank Him!*

Apply:

When you see the word *yet* in scripture, go back and read the section leading up to it because it will help put things in perspective. In this instance, it lets us know the author is making a conscious decision to hold on to his faith in God regardless of the troubles he's seeing around him. Rather than giving in to feelings of hopelessness, he is choosing to trust the Lord no matter what.

That's what you call BIG faith. It's when you choose to put on big-girl pants and make those hard decisions to believe God in spite of your circumstances. It's not letting fear win, or insecurities bloom. It's when you keep your eyes focused directly on God and ignore all the mess swirling around you.

How does this encourage you or challenge you?

Where do you need to have BIG faith right now? Ask God to give you the courage and confidence to trust Him with gusto!

Pray:

God, I need a dose of big faith right now. Sometimes I get bogged down by the hard things around me and I focus on them instead of You. No matter what, I want to have faith like Habakkuk. In Jesus' name I pray. Amen.

God Thinks You're Amazing

Read Zephaniah 3:1–20

Key Verse:

"The LORD your God is in your midst, A Warrior who saves. He will rejoice over you with joy; He will be quiet in His love [making no mention of your past sins], He will rejoice over you with shouts of joy."
ZEPHANIAH 3:17 AMP

Understand:

- *Reread the verse above. What part(s) of it encourages your heart the very most right now? Spend time telling God about it, and thank Him for being your greatest cheerleader no matter what.*
- *What might it look like for God to rejoice over you with joy? Ask Him for insight and journal it out.*

Apply:

This is one of those verses that calms anxious hearts. It offers so much comfort because it tells you some very important things about God. You're reminded that He is with you, that He battles on your behalf, that your very being pleases Him, and that He doesn't keep track of the things you've done wrong in the past.

Know anyone on earth like this? Probably not.

While your friends and family love you and think you're pretty cool, remember that God loves you even more. No one here can come close to feeling the way He does about you. He's a protective, caring, compassionate, and forgiving Father, and He is just crazy about you!

How does it make you feel, knowing the way God thinks about you? Is it easy to believe and accept, or do you struggle to feel worthy of His love and attention? Regardless of how you may feel, God will never change the way He feels because He created you in His image. And God thinks you're amazing.

Pray:

God, sometimes it's hard for me to understand how You can love someone like me. I can be messy and moody and do things that don't glorify Your name. Thank You for loving me anyway. I'm humbled by Your compassion toward me. And I love You back! In Jesus' name I pray. Amen.

When Your Spirit Is Sparked into Action

Read Haggai 1:1–15

Key Verse:

So the LORD sparked the enthusiasm of Zerubbabel son of Shealtiel, governor of Judah, and the enthusiasm of Jeshua son of Jehozadak, the high priest, and the enthusiasm of the whole remnant of God's people. They began to work on the house of their God.
HAGGAI 1:14 NLT

Understand:

- *Can you remember a time God "sparked" you into action? How did you know it was Him?*
- *Where do you need enthusiasm to take the next right step? What is keeping you from moving forward? Have you asked God for what you need?*

Apply:

Sometimes you need God to intervene and spark you into action. You need Him to get you off the couch, change your mind-set, give you enthusiasm, infuse you with courage, or ignite excitement to do something new. With everything on your busy calendar—school, practice, work, friends, family time—you sometimes need an extra push to find the gumption to move forward.

Just like He did for those in today's verse, He will for you too.

Have you ever been too overwhelmed to consider taking something else on or had your your heart set on a lazy weekend to watch Netflix? Maybe you've been afraid to try that thing again because it didn't go so well the first time. Or maybe something seems too difficult and you don't want to risk failing.

Ask God to get you moving! Ask Him for courage, perseverance, or time. Sometimes the very thing you need is the Spirit to spark you into action.

Pray:

God, sometimes I need a heavenly push from You to move forward. And most of the time, I don't even realize that I do. Will You continue to spark my enthusiasm for the things I need to be doing? And will You encourage me to follow Your plan for my life? In Jesus' name I pray. Amen.

Making Your Way Back to God

Read Zechariah 1:1–21

Key Verse:

"So give to the people this Message from GOD-of-the-Angel-Armies: 'Come back to me and I'll come back to you.'"
ZECHARIAH 1:3 MSG

Understand:

- *How is your relationship with God right now? Have you been distant from Him? Has your time with Him been strained? If so, why?*
- *Think about the things you do that help you feel closest to God and write them down. Is it youth group each week or spending one-on-one time with Him? Is it listening to worship music, focusing in on the words? Is it journaling your thoughts and prayers? Something else?*

Apply:

In today's scripture, God's message was clear: come back to me because I'll be here waiting! God promises all throughout His Word that He will never leave you. So, the truth is that if you're feeling distant from God right now, He's not the one who walked away or turned His back on you.

Maybe life has gotten busy with chores, school, work, practice, friends, or a new hobby. Maybe your family has been traveling or you're in the throes of moving. Life will always be busy and you'll always have a to-do list, and unless making time for God is a priority, it will negatively affect your relationship with Him.

Can you imagine going a week without talking to your bestie? Or not seeing your parents for a month? Or missing two games with your teammates? Distance with those we love and care about is hard!

If you're far from God right now, make your way back to Him in those ways you've connected with Him before. He's waiting!

Pray:

God, I'm sorry I've been distant. I didn't mean to walk away from You, but I let life get in the way. Help me keep our relationship a top priority. You matter to me! In Jesus' name I pray. Amen.

Supernatural Dreams

Read Matthew 1:18–2:25

Key Verse:

While he was still debating with himself about what to do, he fell asleep and had a supernatural dream. An angel from the Lord appeared to him in clear light and said, "Joseph, descendant of David, don't hesitate to take Mary into your home as your wife, because the power of the Holy Spirit has conceived a child in her womb."

MATTHEW 1:20 TPT

Understand:

- *How can you know if it's God speaking to you through your dreams?*
- *Fear is not from God. So you can be certain that any nightmares or night terrors are not ways God would ever speak to you. If you're having them, have you asked God for His peace as you sleep?*

Apply:

Experts agree that everyone dreams about one to two hours a night. It's our brain's way of processing the day. But scripture also tells us that God uses dreams to speak to us. So how do you know if your dream is from God?

Because He uses consistent and persistent messages to get our attention, if your dream is the same message you've been hearing from other people and places. . .it might be God. Maybe your pastor preached it on Sunday, your friend gave similar advice, and it was in your daily devotional reading.

Even more, a God-inspired dream will reflect God's character and heart for you. They will help you live a better life, inspire better choices, and will point you to Jesus. If your dreams are full of fear and dread, chances are they are not from God.

Ask Him for discernment so you can know if He's trying to communicate with you through your dreams and visions. And ask for wisdom and clarity so you can understand what He's saying to you through them.

Pray:

God, help me know if You're using dreams to talk to me. I want to hear You loud and clear because Your words matter to me! In Jesus' name I pray. Amen.

Just Love Everyone
Read Matthew 3:1–17

Key Verse:

John wore wild clothes made from camel hair with a leather belt around his waist—the clothes of an outcast, a rebel. He ate locusts and wild honey.
MATTHEW 3:4 VOICE

Understand:

- *If God made everyone different on purpose, why do you think people judge others for being unique? How can you be a support for those who feel like an outcast?*
- *Think about your friends, writing down five distinctive things about them you love. Then find time to sit down and tell them how much you appreciate those things.*

Apply:

For all intents and purposes, John the Baptist was a little whack-a-doo. He dressed differently than others. His diet of bugs wasn't considered the norm of the time (or any time, right?). And scripture even tells us he preached naked. He was eccentric, and there's no doubt people found him to be weird. But none of that disqualified him in God's eyes, because it was God who created the ins and outs of him.

John was fully accepted by God.

Every single one of us battles the urge to judge others in a negative light. It's easy to look at their differences and decide they are unlikable. So often, it's those unique qualities that open people up to being bullied. And that is not cool.

Be someone who celebrates those differences. Teach others to respect that we each have physical qualities worthy of appreciation. And never let yourself join in the crowd when they're making fun of someone.

Pray:

God, help me love and appreciate the differences in others. Give me Your eyes to see them as You do. And allow me to be an agent of change, encouraging those around me to celebrate one another rather than cut them down for being unique. In Jesus' name I pray. Amen.

He Came for You

Read Mark 2:1–17

Key Verse:

When Jesus heard it, he said to them, "Healthy people don't need a doctor, but sick people do. I didn't come to call righteous people, but sinners."

MARK 2:17 CEB

Understand:

- *Jesus often told His Truth through examples or parables. What does this verse mean to you? Do you consider yourself healthy or sick?*
- *Do you think you have to be flawless or blameless to have a relationship with Jesus? Why or why not?*

Apply:

This verse is good news for us! Jesus is saying that He chose to step down from His heavenly throne, wrap Himself in human flesh, all so He could offer hope to anyone who had sin in their lives. And at last check, that's everyone, right?

Sometimes we think we have to clean ourselves up and get our act together before we can reach out to God. We're ashamed of our past or our current season of sinning, and so we hide away rather than develop a relationship with Him.

You don't have to have perfect grades or be on the Varsity team. You don't have to have a perfect track record of good choices or be a flawless Christian. Being part of the popular crowd at school or having the best summer job in town doesn't matter. Jesus came to earth because He loved you!

Tell God those things that keep you from accepting His unconditional love, and then ask Him to give you the courage and confidence to embrace it! When Jesus says He came to earth for you, He meant exactly that. You were worth the trip from heaven!

Pray:

God, I'm so glad You don't expect me to be perfect. Thank You for choosing to come to earth and for loving me in all my glorious mess. Help me receive the gift of Your unchangeable love, especially in those moments I feel unlovable. In Jesus' name I pray. Amen.

Jesus Was Tempted Too

Read Luke 4:1–16

Key Verse:

For 40 days, the Spirit led Him from place to place in the desert, and while there, the devil tempted Jesus. Jesus was fasting, eating nothing during this time, and at the end, He was terribly hungry.
LUKE 4:2 VOICE

Understand:

- *What are your greatest temptations? What are those places that are the hardest to say no to? How might talking to Jesus about them help?*
- *Jesus was tempted relentlessly. Scripture says there's no temptation He hasn't faced. How can this truth bring comfort to your struggles?*

Apply:

We face temptations of all kinds. Just think about what's tried to get your attention this week alone. Maybe it's been a temptation to lie or cheat. Maybe it was to sneak out of your house or deliberately break curfew. It might have been to use bad language or talk back to authority. Or maybe it was to eat the whole box of cookies or watch something inappropriate on television.

There are no shortages of temptations. There are opportunities galore to make bad choices. Why not talk to Jesus about them?

If He could withstand—as a human—forty days of temptation on an empty stomach. . .wouldn't you think He might be someone who could give you strength and wisdom to withstand what you're facing right now?

He knows the world you live in and all of the curiosities that come with it. He knows what interests you and what things attract your attention. He knows those lures that make it hard to choose the right path. And if you ask, He will help you overcome them all.

Pray:

God, I really appreciate knowing that Jesus faced temptations just like I do. Because of that, He knows how hard it can be to choose the right way. And I'm so glad to know I can ask Him for help to make good choices. In Jesus' name I pray. Amen.

Be a Good Friend

Read Luke 5:12–26

Key Verse:

*But finding no way to bring him in because of
the crowd, they went up on the roof [and removed
some tiles to make an opening] and lowered him
through the tiles with his stretcher, into the
middle of the crowd, in front of Jesus.*
LUKE 5:19 AMP

Understand:

- *Think about what qualities you like most
  in your friends. What are the things they
  do for you, the way they treat you, or the
  encouragement they offer that means the
  most?*
- *There's an aspect of servanthood in
  friendship. It's the choice to put others
  before you, making sure their needs are
  known and met. What does this look like
  in your relationships?*

Apply:

Talk about good friends! Can you even imagine the
time and effort it took for these men to hoist their
friend to the roof, create a big enough hole for him

to fit through, and then gently lower him into the room and in front of Jesus? Their compassion and care for him offers us a beautiful example of what good friends look like.

What part of this story means the most to you? Is it that this disabled man had a group to call his own? Maybe it's that they went up and above the call of duty to help him out? Is it that they weren't afraid to cause a commotion to help him? Something else?

God created you for community, which means you have a built-in desire to connect with others. There's something so powerful about being surrounded by people who love you and believe in you.

Decide to make friends who encourage you to be the best you. And be that kind of friend right back.

Pray:

God, thank You for putting people in my life who love me well. Would You give me wisdom to continue choosing good friends in life, and would You help me be the best kind of friend to others? In Jesus' name I pray. Amen.

Stand Up for Others

Read Luke 23:13–43

Key Verse:

A great crowd gathered to watch what was happening.
The religious leaders sneered at Jesus and mocked
him, saying, "Look at this man! What kind of
'chosen Messiah' is this? He pretended to save
others, but he can't even save himself!"
LUKE 23:35 TPT

Understand:

- *Can you remember a time you were mocked or bullied? Did anyone come to your rescue? Did you advocate for yourself? What did you learn from that experience?*
- *Why do you think certain people make fun of others? What might be the benefit they receive? What might it say about how they feel about themselves?*

Apply:

Jesus was hanging on the cross, dying. He had been betrayed by Judas, denied by Peter, and now the religious leaders were mocking Him publicly. No one boldly faced His accusers and stood up for Him. He had a few, but those supporting Him were few and far between. Think how lonely Jesus must have felt in that moment.

Think about your own life. Have you ever felt like there was no one was in your corner? Maybe some mean girls or jeering boys were focusing in on you and nobody was around to help. Maybe you were bullied for your faith or morals, and you were left standing alone.

Or maybe you were the one to mock someone else.

Decide today that you will stand up for those targeted by bullies. Surround yourself with friends who won't tolerate the mocking of others. Be someone willing to stand up for kindness and respect at all costs. And know that with Jesus' help, you can do it.

Pray:

God, it's hard to know how much hate Jesus faced while on earth. I want to be a voice of change so that kind of harsh treatment doesn't happen to me, around me, or by me. Give me courage to stand up for what's right. Give me strength to speak up. In Jesus' name I pray. Amen.

We've All Sinned and Fallen Short

Read John 8:1–30

Key Verse:

However, when they persisted in questioning Him, He straightened up and said, "He who is without [any] sin among you, let him be the first to throw a stone at her."

JOHN 8:7 AMP

Understand:

- *Do you have a measuring stick for sin, deciding some are worse than others? Do you know someone who does? How can this be a dangerous practice?*
- *Vulnerability is attractive. There's something beautiful about someone willing to share their struggles and challenges. What does this look like in your life and relationships?*

Apply:

Have you ever looked at your mess-ups and decided they're not as bad as their mess-ups? It's easy to look at someone else's sins and think you're better than them. You may decide you're smarter, holier, nicer, wiser, or more worthy of love. You may think, "Well at least I didn't do *that*!" Maybe your sin is hidden while their sin is public, so it naturally makes you look like your life is all together.

The temptation is to ignore the parts of your heart and life you need to work on, justifying your sin. But that's not God's hope for you.

The Bible says there is no condemnation in Christ. Admitting your sin doesn't make you bad or unlovable. It just makes you right with God. It removes any barrier in your relationship with Him so you can live your best life together.

Before pointing your finger at others, ask God to help you see your own struggles. And ask God for compassion, realizing everyone makes mistakes.

Pray:

God, I don't want to think I'm better than anyone.
Instead, I want to be willing to look at my own
messiness and be a support to others in theirs.
We're all in this life together, right? Help me
be a good friend to everyone around me.
In Jesus' name I pray. Amen.

Keep Your Eyes on God

Read Acts 7:1–60

Key Verse:

But Stephen, overtaken with great faith, was full of the Holy Spirit. He fixed his gaze into the heavenly realm and saw the glory and splendor of God—and Jesus, who stood up at the right hand of God.

Acts 7:55 TPT

Understand:

- *How would your heart and perspective be different if you chose to focus on God rather than look at the scary and frustrating circumstances you're facing?*
- *Every day you have the freedom to choose how to respond to life's ups and downs with friendships, schoolwork, family, and responsibilities. Where do you need to make different choices?*

Apply:

Stephen's circumstances were not good. He'd been sharing God's story, and it angered a mob who took him outside the city and stoned him to death. But rather than be overwhelmed by the situation, Stephen's faith increased and He gazed into the heavens and fixed his eyes on God.

What tough circumstances are you facing right now? Maybe you've had a fallout with a friend, are at odds with a parent, aren't seeing eye-to-eye with a coach, or got fired from a job. These are the kinds of things that can take you out, keeping you sad or angry at the world. They can ruin your day and make you want to hide under your covers.

What if instead, you looked past your circumstances and focused on God. Rather than wallow you prayed? Rather than replaying the moment over and over again in your mind, you opened the Bible? What if you chose to believe God's promises more than any fear created by the mess you're in?

Pray:

God, I want to focus on You more than my circumstances. I want to keep my eyes focused on You, Lord! And remind me that I can get through anything with Your help. In Jesus' name I pray. Amen.

Don't Be Ashamed to Share Jesus

Read Romans 1:1–32

Key Verse:

*I refuse to be ashamed of sharing the wonderful message
of God's liberating power unleashed in us through
Christ! For I am thrilled to preach that everyone
who believes is saved—the Jew first,
and then people everywhere!*
ROMANS 1:16 TPT

Understand:

- *How would you respond if someone asked
  you to share your faith in Jesus or your
  personal testimony with a group of people
  from your school or community? Would
  you be excited to share? Why or why not?*
- *If someone were to ask your friends,
  classmates, or teammates if you're a Jesus
  follower, what would they say?*

Apply:

It can be terrifying to share your faith with others.
Part of it may be that you're shy or feel uncomfort-
able talking in a group, but it could also be scary
because telling others about your belief in Jesus is a
vulnerable act.

And vulnerability can sometimes feel unsafe.

Even more, the world often seems hostile to the idea of following God. So finding the courage to open up and expose your faith may feel like being a seal in shark-infested waters. And it's that fear of rejection that convinces you to keep your mouth shut and your faith hidden.

But sweet one, please don't let fear or insecurity keep you in hiding. You're part of God's Plan A to share Him with the world. He's counting on your words and actions to point others to Him. And in those times where you need the courage to speak up, He will give it to you when you ask. Guaranteed.

Pray:

God, I don't want to hide my faith. I don't want to be scared to share You with my friends. Please grow confidence in me so I'm able to be bold in sharing how much I love You! In Jesus' name I pray. Amen.

How You Live Matters

Read 1 Corinthians 10:1–33

Key Verse:

Whether you eat or drink, live your life in
a way that glorifies and honors God.
1 CORINTHIANS 10:31 TPT

Understand:

- *What do you think it means to live in a*
  way that glorifies and honors God? Who
  are your family and friends who live this
  verse out loud?
- *God is asking that your entire life be on*
  display so others will see Him because
  of how you live. What would have to
  change in your words or actions to make
  this happen?

Apply:

In today's verse, Paul is encouraging the church in Corinth to be mindful of how they live. . .because it matters. He's reminding them that their goal—and our goal—should be to glorify and honor the Lord with how we live.

Your choices and decisions carry weight with your friends. And because you're a Jesus girl, people watch how you live your life. Spreading rumors at school, cheating on tests, sneaking out, lying to parents, ignoring others, using curse words, being meanspirited, causing drama, and treating teachers or parents rudely does nothing to promote the Lord to those around you.

If asked, would your teachers and classmates know you love the Lord? Would they notice that you are kind and compassionate toward others? Would you be known as a stinker or a person who tries to live the right life? When in trouble or struggling with something, would you be a safe place?

This isn't a call to be perfect. It's an invitation to live with purpose. Are you up for it?

Pray:

God, I want my life to point to You. I want others to know You because of the choices I make. Help me be a poster child for You, Lord! What an honor and privilege that You'd ask me to share my faith with those around me. In Jesus' name I pray. Amen.

It's All about Perspective

Read 2 Corinthians 4:1–18

Key Verse:

We view our slight, short-lived troubles in the light of eternity. We see our difficulties as the substance that produces for us an eternal, weighty glory far beyond all comparison.
2 CORINTHIANS 4:17 TPT

Understand:

- *Think about how you react to a tough situation. Do you see it for what it is, or do you pull out the drama-queen crown and place it squarely on your head? Where did you learn this behavior?*
- *John 16:33 says that in this life you will have trouble. So knowing that, why do you think He'd allow those painful and messy moments? What are they good for?*

Apply:

What an eternal perspective! Paul refuses to see any struggle or challenge that comes his way in a negative light. Instead, he understands that God has allowed them for a powerful purpose. What about you?

When your boyfriend dumps you, or your bestie

shares your secret. . .when your parents ground you or the coach cuts you from the team. . .when your boss fires you, or you don't get picked for the musical. . . what's your response?

This is where you get to choose how you see these tough situations. You can trust that God allowed it because He'll use it for His glory and your benefit. Or you can go into drama mode, throwing the best pity party in the history of the world.

One way highlights your faith, and the other exposes the lack of it. One way shows an eternal perspective and the other reveals a worldly, selfish view.

Getting hurt, being scared, and facing a letdown are normal responses to life. But it's what you choose to do with those that matters.

Pray:

God, it's hard to be brave when bad things happen. Sometimes I want to throw a fit rather than be strong. Will You help me see the messy times with an eternal perspective rather than an earthly one? In Jesus' name I pray. Amen.

Be Fruity!
Read Galatians 5:1–26

Key Verse:

*But the fruit produced by the Holy Spirit within you
is divine love in all its varied expressions: joy that
overflows, peace that subdues, patience that endures,
kindness in action, a life full of virtue, faith that
prevails, gentleness of heart, and strength of
spirit. Never set the law above these qualities,
for they are meant to be limitless.*
GALATIANS 5:22-23 TPT

Understand:

- *Think about the fruits of the Spirit.
  Which ones do you see in your life right
  now? Which ones do you need the Holy
  Spirit to grow in you?*
- *How do you think the Spirit grows these
  fruits in you? What can you do to help the
  process? What could you do to hinder it?*

Apply:

Being a Jesus girl has benefits. One of them is being
gifted with the fruits of the Spirit. These gifts are
cultivated in you through the Holy Spirit's supervi-
sion, and these fruits are meant to not only benefit

you. . .but others as well. These take time to grow to maturity—just as all good things do—but you can access them when you need them now.

Sometimes we think we're fully responsible for mustering up these gifts ourselves. We place the burden on us to make these a part of our everyday lives. But we are not God. And when we struggle to have joy, have lost our peace, are short on patience and kindness, can't grab onto faith, and have abandoned love and gentleness toward others, we feel like failures.

Be careful to not set unrealistic expectations for yourself. You're not the gardener. But you can practice using these fruits in your friendships right now. And when you find one that needs to mature more, ask God to help!

Pray:

God, thank You for the fruits of the Spirit. And thank You that I'm not responsible for developing these myself. Would You help me be aware of what fruits need maturing so I can be the best version of me to my friends and family? In Jesus' name I pray. Amen.

Armor Up!

Read Ephesians 6:10–20

Key Verse:

*Put on God's complete set of armor provided for us,
so that you will be protected as you fight against
the evil strategies of the accuser!*
EPHESIANS 6:11 TPT

Understand:

- *After reading about the armor of God,
  which piece(s) stood out to you the most?
  What piece(s) was new to you? Which
  piece(s) did you not realize you needed?*
- *Why do you think it's important to armor
  up? What/who does it help protect you
  from? What might happen if you don't
  put it on every day?*

Apply:

In today's reading, Paul tells us that our struggles really aren't with people. Of course, they can make us mad and hurt our feelings, but he goes to on to say that the true battle we face is with the enemy. He and his minions are behind the evil we see in the world.

Because you are so loved, God created a set of divine armor that you can access. The belt of truth, the breastplate of righteousness, your feet fitted with the Gospel of peace, the shield of faith, the helmet of salvation, and the sword of the Spirit are designed to protect you against the schemes of the devil.

Don't be afraid of him, and don't focus your energy on him either. The enemy is not worth your time. But do be aware that he's working behind the scenes to discourage you at every turn. And the coolest thing is that God's already taken care of that. His armor will give you the edge over the devil every time.

Pray:

God, You think of everything. I will put on Your armor every day so I can be ready to face whatever the enemy brings my way. I will not fear him, because You're my Father and have already made a way for me to be victorious! In Jesus' name I pray. Amen.

When You're Worried. . .Pray!

Read Philippians 4:1–23

Key Verse:

Don't be pulled in different directions or worried about a thing. Be saturated in prayer throughout each day, offering your faith-filled requests before God with overflowing gratitude. Tell him every detail of your life.
PHILIPPIANS 4:6 TPT

Understand:

- *What are the things that worry you the most? Make a list, then tell God about everything you wrote down. Listen for His responses, and consider writing them next to the concerns you shared with Him so you can revisit them when that stress pops up again.*
- *Reread today's Key Verse. How do Paul's words challenge you to shift your perspective and change how you react to the things that cause worry?*

Apply:

What's the antidote to worry? Prayer. Did you realize how very powerful prayer can be as a weapon in your arsenal?

What is your usual response to anxiety? Do you talk to your friends about it? Journal it out? Tell a trusted family member? Go into meltdown mode? Respond in anger, lashing out at those you love? Stress eat? Hide in bed? Chances are you have lots of different reactions when you're frazzled.

But in the middle of all these options, have you ever just sat down and prayed? Have you ever cried out to God in your pain? Have you shared your fears with Him? Well, guess what. He wants to hear you share every single detail of the situations that stress you out. God is never too busy or too burdened to give you His full attention.

And even more, He has exactly what you need to navigate through the concerns that weigh heavily on your heart.

Pray:

God, there are so many things that make me nervous right now. I am scared and stressed and unable to handle them all on my own. Will You please help me? I need You. In Jesus' name I pray. Amen.

Forgiving Frees You
Read Colossians 3:1–25

Key Verse:

Tolerate the weaknesses of those in the family of faith, forgiving one another in the same way you have been graciously forgiven by Jesus Christ. If you find fault with someone, release this same gift of forgiveness to them.
COLOSSIANS 3:13 TPT

Understand:

- *What are the things that worry you the most? Make a list, then tell God about everything you wrote down. Listen for His response, and consider writing them next to the concerns you shared with Him so you can revisit them when that stress pops up again.*
- *Reread today's Key Verse. How do Paul's words challenge you to shift your perspective and change how you react to the things that cause worry?*

Apply:

Sometimes we choose not to forgive because we think doing so lets the other person off the hook for hurting us. We think that forgiving means the pain we felt wasn't real and that the meanspirited things they did to us—intentionally or not—weren't rude or wrong. But none of those are true. Those are lies that keep us trapped in unforgiveness.

Here's some powerful truth. When you choose to forgive someone, it 100 percent benefits you because holding on to an offense traps you in a prison—one you cannot get out of.

Think about how much time you spent replaying the mean words your friend said to you, or revisiting the hurt you felt for not being invited to the party. Did those moments slowly begin to overtake your thoughts, and the memories hurt you over and over and over again? Holding on to that unforgiveness imprisoned you, whether you knew it or not.

Be quick to forgive. Let it go, and live free!

Pray:

God, I've been believing lies that have trapped me in the prison of unforgiveness. Help me remember that forgiving others benefits me the most, allowing me to focus on the good things in my life. In Jesus' name I pray. Amen.

Be a Voice of Encouragement

Read 1 Thessalonians 5:1–28

Key Verse:

*So speak encouraging words to one another.
Build up hope so you'll all be together in this,
no one left out, no one left behind. I know
you're already doing this; just keep on doing it.*
1 THESSALONIANS 5:11 MSG

Understand:

- *What kinds of affirmation do you need
  to hear the most? Who are the people
  who speak those to you on the regular?
  How can you let them know how much it
  means?*
- *Is there someone who could really use a
  text or note of encouragement from you
  today? Ask God to give you the right
  words to share with them.*

Apply:

In a world where people can be mean for sport,
choose to be someone who is generous with their
encouragement. Everyone is quick to tell you all
you're doing wrong and what you need to fix or
change. And with all the negativity floating around,

sometimes a kind word can make all the difference in a friend's day.

Maybe the new kid needs an invitation to sit with you at lunch, or your teacher needs a note that tells her how much she's appreciated. Maybe your server at the restaurant needs to know they did a good job, or the store cashier needs a *thank you*. Chances are Mom could use an *I love you*, and complimenting your grandmother's hairdo would make her smile. Everyone needs encouragement.

So decide to be a cheerleader, always on the lookout for opportunities to inspire and motivate those around you every day. It may be exactly what someone needs!

Pray:

God, I want to be a bright light in the lives of those around me. I want to be someone who is kind and generous with words of hope. And I need Your help to live this out every day. Please use my words and actions to inspire and affirm others. In Jesus' name I pray. Amen.

You Are Who You Hang Out With

Read 2 Thessalonians 3:1–28

Key Verse:

*Beloved brothers and sisters, we instruct you,
in the name of our Lord Jesus Christ, to stay away
from believers who are unruly and who stray
from all that we have taught you.*
2 Thessalonians 3:6 TPT

Understand:

- *Think about your group of friends.
  Do they influence you to do the right
  things or do they tempt you to disobey
  your parents or the law? Are there some
  changes that need to be made?*
- *What kind of influence are you on those
  you hang out with?*

Apply:

It's so true. You are who you hang out with, which
can be super awesome or not good at all. It's very
common for a friend's idiosyncrasies, catch phrases,
interests, likes and dislikes, manners, thought pat-
terns, and focuses to rub off on you. That's why it's
so important to make sure you choose your friends
wisely.

Even more, make sure that you're a good influence on others too! How you live your life speaks loudly and has the power to encourage your friends to be their best selves.

Be a focused student. Treat others with kindness. Don't gossip or bully. Live out your faith. Extend grace and forgive. Hold to your morals. Respect authority. Honor your parents. Be nice to your siblings. Make wise choices. Don't let fear rule you. Be a good sport.

Make sure you're the kind of person who calls their friends higher, and make an intentional decision to be around people who do the same for you.

Pray:

God, I know it matters who I hang out with.
Help me be wise when choosing my friends, and quick
to walk away if their influence isn't good for me.
Also, give me the confidence and discernment
to be a moral inspiration for others too.
In Jesus' name I pray. Amen.

Your Age Doesn't Matter

Read 1 Timothy 4:8–16

Key Verse:

And don't be intimidated by those who are older than you; simply be the example they need to see by being faithful and true in all that you do. Speak the truth and live a life of purity and authentic love as you remain strong in your faith.
1 Timothy 4:12 TPT

Understand:

- *How does your age affect how others think about you and your abilities? Do you feel like others see your talents and giftings regardless?*
- *Do you think it's possible to be a role model no matter how old you are? Who are your role models? Who looks up to you?*

Apply:

Don't ever let anyone tell you that your age is a deficit. You may not have lived as much life as those older than you, but you can still be a powerful force for good in the world. You can still be a beacon of hope for your generation. You can still have a voice of influence for the kingdom.

Never apologize for being who God made you to be.

And think about this. He decided now would be the perfect time on the kingdom calendar for you to be alive. God packed you full of gifts that the world needs at this moment. He placed a call on your life to be walked out right now. You are a mighty purpose, sweet one.

So be a faithful daughter and friend, and be known as a truth teller. Make sure your life is marked with good decisions and choices. Choose purity. And be a lover of people, sharing kindness and compassion at every turn.

Pray:

God, I'm encouraged to live well no matter my age. I want to be a force for You on earth in all I say and do. I know I won't do this perfectly, but help me do it with purpose. In Jesus' name I pray. Amen.

Fear Is Not from God

Read 2 Timothy 1:1–18

Key Verse:

For God did not give us a spirit of timidity or cowardice or fear, but [He has given us a spirit] of power and of love and of sound judgment and personal discipline [abilities that result in a calm, well-balanced mind and self-control].

2 TIMOTHY 1:7 AMP

Understand:

- *If fear doesn't come from God, where does it come from? What has it stolen from you?*
- *Think about all the things that scare you. Talk to God about them, and ask for Him to replace them with power, love, and sound judgment.*

Apply:

This is one of the most power-packed verses in the Bible because it speaks directly about fear. Maybe fear is your constant companion and you don't even realize it controls your choices and decisions. Maybe you're very aware of your fear but don't know how to get past it.

It's important to remember that God will never use fear to punish or direct your next step. But the enemy will. As a matter of fact, it's his greatest weapon designed to stop you right in your tracks.

Fear tells you to give up. It says you can't do something so don't even try. It reminds you of all the times you failed and of every embarrassing moment. Fear says you're not good enough, lovable enough, smart enough, wise enough, liked enough, pretty enough, and every other *not enough* you can think of.

But God says you can. You will. You're awesome. And you are enough! So friend, don't let fear run your life anymore.

Pray:

God, I don't want fear to rule me. It's a liar that has run my life way too long. Would You please give me the courage and confidence to live out the purposes You have for my life? In Jesus' name I pray. Amen.

Let Go and Move On

Read Hebrews 12:1–29

Key Verse:

As for us, we have all of these great witnesses who encircle us like clouds. So we must let go of every wound that has pierced us and the sin we so easily fall into. Then we will be able to run life's marathon race with passion and determination, for the path has been already marked out before us.
HEBREWS 12:1 TPT

Understand:

- *If fear doesn't come from God, where does it come from? What has it stolen from you?*
- *Think about all the things that scare you. Talk to God about them and ask for Him to replace them with power, love, and sound judgment.*

Apply:

It's common—but not a good strategy—to collect our hurts and carry them around with us. We collect things like mean comments or a friend's betrayal. We collect times we felt rejected or unaccepted by others. We collect failures and fallouts. And sometimes we use them to justify our poor-me mentality, hoping that others will feel sorry for us.

But you know what hoarding them really does? It causes you to lose sight of the awesome plans God created just for you. You get tangled up in all that's bad and wrong, and you stop living with passion and purpose.

Sweet one, God wants to heal those hurts so you can let go of them. And when you do that, you're supernaturally freed up to run the race He has set before you with joy and determination! It doesn't mean you won't remember those hard, messy times, but they won't have power over you anymore.

Pray:

God, I don't want to collect my wounds because they won't do me any good. Instead, would You please heal me so they can't affect my love of life any longer? I want to be full of joy and enjoy my life, friends, and family! In Jesus' name I pray. Amen.

Consider It Joy?

Read James 1

Key Verse:

*My fellow believers, when it seems as though you are
facing nothing but difficulties see it as an invaluable
opportunity to experience the greatest joy that you can!*
JAMES 1:2 TPT

Understand:

- *What would it take to change how you
  think about those hard moments in life—
  seeing them as helpful instead of horrible?*
- *Think about the last rough season of life
  you went through. Did you lean on God
  or did you give in to despair?*

Apply:

Have you ever wondered just how the heck you're
supposed live out today's Key Verse? How is a broken
friendship, a failing grade, a losing season, a scream-
ing match, parents' divorce, a grandparent's death, a
school change, or a scary diagnosis an opportunity
for joy?

Many agree this is super challenging because it
doesn't feel normal or natural to see sad and messy
moments as opportunities for anything more than

throwing a good ole temper tantrum. Amen? And it's because of that, you have to understand that you'll absolutely need God's help to do it.

On your own, finding this kind of eternal perspective feels hopeless. But in these times, cry out to God and ask Him to increase your faith so you can trust His plans. Ask Him to comfort you and bring peace.

And don't forget to ask God to restore your joy—not joy that bad things happened, but joy that He will get you through it.

Pray:

God I'll be honest, finding joy in the heartaches of life feels like a tall order. It feels like something I'll never be able to do on my own. So, I'm glad to know that You will meet me in those times and help me see that there is hope and that You have a perfect plan. In Jesus' name I pray. Amen.

This Is Who You Really Are

Read 1 Peter 2:1–25

Key Verse:

*But you are a chosen race, a royal priesthood,
a consecrated nation, a [special] people for God's
own possession, so that you may proclaim the
excellencies [the wonderful deeds and virtues
and perfections] of Him who called you out
of darkness into His marvelous light.*

1 PETER 2:9 AMP

Understand:

- *Do you allow negative self-talk? What
  are the mean-spirited messages you tell
  yourself? Ask God what He thinks of you.*
- *How do you think God sees you? Do you
  think He loves you no matter what? Or
  do you think His love is dependent on
  your actions? What is the truth?*

Apply:

Who does the world say that you are? Chances are
you hear plenty of messages full of *not good enough*
and *if only* comments, leaving you to doubt your
lovability. And sometimes, those messages can be so
loud.

But you know what else? We can often be the ones whispering lies of worthlessness to our own selves. Sometimes we're our worst critic. But God must have known the tendency we'd have to beat ourselves up, so He made sure to include scriptures reminding us who we really are.

Take a moment to let this sink in: you are *chosen*, you are *royalty*, you are *special*, and you are God's. When He created you, He filled your heart with love and your mind with wisdom. He made you with gifts and talents like no one else, and you have God's stamp of approval.

That means you don't need it from anyone else. You are 100 percent loved and accepted because You are His.

Pray:

God, help me stand in the truth of who I am. Sometimes the world's voice is so loud and I hear the negative more than the positive. But I don't want to live that way. I want to believe I am who You say I am. In Jesus' name I pray. Amen.

No One Is Perfect

Read 1 John 1:1–10

Key Verse:

*If we boast that we have no sin, we're only fooling
ourselves and are strangers to the truth.*
1 JOHN 1:8 TPT

Understand:

- *Would you say that it's hard for you to
admit you are wrong, or that you've done
something wrong? Do you think God
expects you to be flawless? Do you think
others do? Why or why not?*
- *What would you muster the courage to
try if you weren't afraid to fail or mess
up? How can you learn to set aside your
imperfections and try anyway?*

Apply:

Somewhere along the way, we decided that being
honest about our mess-ups was a bad thing. We
became scared to admit failures or flubs and instead
wanted to present ourselves as perfect to those
around us.

Maybe we're afraid of being judged or ridiculed
by others. Maybe we think that our lovability is based

on our performance. Maybe we're so insecure, certain that our flaws only confirm the lie we're believing that says we're not good enough. Or maybe we have unrealistic expectations for ourselves—ones we can't possibly live up to.

Sweet one, God isn't expecting you to be perfect. Jesus is—and will always be—the only unflawed person to walk on planet earth. Instead, God wants you to live with purpose and passion. He wants you to try, knowing you'll fail at times. He wants you to live the adventure without being worried that you're defective or damaged.

So, don't hide your human condition. It's okay to not be perfect, because no one is.

Pray:

God, thank You for the reminder that it's okay to be imperfect. Thank You for loving me no matter what. Help me learn to accept that the goal isn't to be flawless and that I am lovable regardless. What a huge relief! In Jesus' name I pray. Amen.

Keep Your Eyes Open
Read Jude 1:1–25

Key Verse:

For certain people have crept in unnoticed [just as if they were sneaking in by a side door]. They are ungodly persons whose condemnation was predicted long ago, for they distort the grace of our God into decadence and immoral freedom [viewing it as an opportunity to do whatever they want], and deny and disown our only Master and Lord, Jesus Christ.
Jude 1:4 AMP

Understand:

- *Can you think of a time you justified an action you would've never considered doing before. . .just because of peer pressure? How is that a slippery slope?*
- *How have you seen the Key Verse play out in your school, in your community, and in the world lately? How can you protect yourself?*

Apply:

Be mindful of those you allow to influence you. We're usually quick to notice when someone says something or does something that's miles apart from what we believe is good and right. But it's harder to see when it's an ever-so-slight deviation from truth.

It may be a simple encouragement to cheat on a test or sneak out for the party. It could be a suggestion to tell a little lie to your parents or play innocent rather than admit fault and accept the natural consequences. These small tweaks in how you live can often seem like no big deal, but they matter to God.

Friend, be aware of whose advice you take. Be conscious of whose suggestions you follow. Make sure your decisions and choices line up with what God wants for you. Ask yourself *would this make Him happy*? If the answer is no, walk away knowing He'll honor your desire to do right.

Pray:

God, please give me the eyes and ears to know when I'm about to compromise my morals and values. I need discernment to see right from wrong, and the courage to make the best choice. In Jesus' name I pray. Amen.

Model the Good

Read 3 John 1

Key Verse:

Friend, don't go along with evil. Model the good.
The person who does good does God's work.
The person who does evil falsifies God,
doesn't know the first thing about God.
3 John 1:11 MSG

Understand:

- *Think about the role peer pressure plays in your life. Do you find it hard to stay strong when everyone is trying to make you compromise your morals or values? If not, what helps you make the hard choice to stay true to your beliefs?*
- *Who are the people you look up to? What do you like about them? What can you learn from them so you can be a role model for others?*

Apply:

Whether you realize it or not, your life preaches. The words you use, the things you do, how you respond to the ups and downs of life are all watched by others. And when they know you are a Jesus girl, your responses tell those around you about God.

How do you react when you get benched or when the teacher calls you out in front of the class? When your friend group dumps you or tells your secrets to others, how do you respond? When your parents are known as the "strict" parents or your sibling isn't liked at school, how do you handle it?

Make no mistake, your actions preach. But don't think you have to be perfect, because that kind of pressure just sets you up for failure. Instead, God is asking you to be mindful, aware that you have an amazing opportunity to point others to Him with your life.

Whenever possible, choose to model the good.

Pray:

God, please use my life to bring others to know You. I want my words and actions to glorify Your holy name because You're worthy of all praise. Thank You for being amazing, Lord! In Jesus' name I pray. Amen.

The Power of Your Story

Read Revelation 12:1-18

Key Verse:

They conquered him completely through the blood of the Lamb and the powerful word of his testimony. They triumphed because they did not love and cling to their own lives, even when faced with death.
REVELATION 12:11 TPT

Understand:

- *What are some of the favorite stories you've heard that deeply encouraged you? What is their common theme?*
- *Think about the times God showed up in your tough or scary situation. Have you documented those in a journal, in an app on your phone, or in your Bible? Consider writing them down so when the hard times hit, you'll have reminders to trust God. . .again.*

Apply:

This may be a challenging book and chapter to read and understand, but one thing is crystal clear: the blood Jesus spilled on the cross for your salvation plus your story of how He has shown up in your life are a powerful combination.

Stories are compelling motivators that help remind you that you can trust your heavenly Father with whatever you're facing right now. Doesn't it comfort you to know others have walked a similar path as you. . .and survived? These accounts grow hope that you'll be okay in the end, and that everything will work out one way or another.

Can you remember a time you were encouraged to take that leap of faith because you heard someone talk about their own? Or inspired by a friend's testimony who was finally able to overcome her insecurities by choosing to believe who God said she is instead of listening to others?

Stories carry weight. Listen to them and share them whenever you need a reminder of God's goodness.

Pray:

God, thank You for the Word because it's stacked full of Your stories that promise to encourage me when I need it the most! Thank You for the willingness of others to share their moving experiences too. And would You give me the courage to share mine when the time is right? In Jesus' name I pray. Amen.

About the Author

Carey Scott is an author, speaker, and certified Biblical Life Coach who is honest about her walk with the Lord—stumbles, fumbles, and all. Through her books *Untangled, Uncommon,* and *Unafraid,* she challenges women to embrace authentic living even when it's messy. And she's a passionate advocate for all women becoming boldly confident in who God says they are.

Carey lives in Colorado with her two kids who give her plenty of epic material for writing and speaking. She's surrounded by a wonderful family and group of friends who keep her motivated, real, and humble. Learn more at CareyScott.org.